The Healing Metaphor

Hypnotherapy Scripts

Zetta Thomelin

Grosvenor House
Publishing Limited

First Edition

Front cover picture copyright Evelyn Meyer
Back cover author photo copyright John Jacques

This book is published by
Grosvenor House Publishing Ltd
Link House
140 The Broadway, Tolworth, Surrey, KT6 7HT.
www.grosvenorhousepublishing.co.uk

The author can be contacted at www.headtogether.net

A CIP record for this book
is available from the British Library

ISBN 978-1-78623-140-6

With thanks to Barbara Thomelin and Evelyn Meyer for their patient proof reading and their support, also thanks go to my two mentors Dr Philippa Berry and Maureen Williams for their encouragement in all my endeavours.

Contents

Why use Metaphors?

A metaphor is a way of communicating an idea in an imaginative rather than a literal way, it harnesses the power of our imagination to pass the message from one mind to another, perhaps a very different mind, but no matter how different we are, the metaphors reach through the difference and deliver.

Metaphor in daily life

I wonder if you have noticed how often we use metaphors in our daily speech. When you do you start to notice it, it is amazing just how littered our daily communications are with metaphors. It is something we are familiar with and use to give greater emphasis to a statement. We might say, "you can see the light at the end of the tunnel" instead of things are going to get better. We say it because it is more powerful, more intense in meaning, it creates resonance and depth, the phrase gives that sudden moment of deep understanding to which everyone can relate, the picture language within the statement is empowering. Let's just look at a few metaphors from current daily speech:

- Let sleeping dogs lie
- You cannot see the wood for the trees
- Don't put all your eggs in one basket
- Swimming against the tide
- Hit the nail on the head
- A level playing field
- Don't look a gift horse in the mouth
- Long in the tooth
- Sailing too close to the wind
- Fallen off the wagon
- Putting your foot in it
- Having several irons in the fire

All of these metaphors speak to us directly and accurately, there is no room for misunderstanding, they are concise and direct, whilst in another sense they are veiled. Each language has it's own metaphors, poetic stories that communicate meaning in an empowered way and often those metaphors are similar, perhaps they could be coming up from the universal unconscious. It is interesting to note that the origins of most of our common metaphors come from way back in time; these sayings are a historical footnote that stays resonant in our language from generation to generation, we hand them down, like hand me down clothes, to enrich our communication and understanding.

A metaphor often builds around it a story. We humans love stories, they are the oldest kind of entertainment, such as in ancient times when people came together around a roaring fire, gathering to listen to the roaming story teller. We then evolved into telling the stories in theatres and we put stories in print to read and then came film and TV, often these stories entertain us educate us, inform us and change us. The old story tellers of past times who walked the land were not just tale tellers but educators and healers, they understood the power of story and the language that painted the picture for the listener. They gave us the epic tales of old, loaded with metaphor and teaching. We understand stories, we can settle down and listen, it is hard wired into our DNA, to enjoy and expect something from a story.

Metaphor in therapy

Metaphors create this special communication partly because they reflect universal truths, that is why metaphors are a powerful tool to utilise in therapy, everyone can relate to them, it gives the subconscious mind that eureka moment of understanding and it leads towards transformation and change. What is also important about the metaphor is its subtlety, it slips between the cracks in the resistant subconscious mind, by using a metaphor in therapy we remove that element of resistance within the client who does not want to be told what to do, it is a stealthy message slipping past the conscious mind into the receptive subconscious/unconscious, unchallenged by the client's critical faculty, just like concealing the medicine for a pet within their food.

We harness the power of the imagination with metaphor and it becomes magical, it evokes synergies and compels understanding in the subconscious mind. The transformative power of story-telling has been used for centuries by the ancient Druids, the Egyptian priests and the early Christians. The relationship between stories and the subtle nature of change, empowers the metaphor for use within therapy and it is familiar to us as a means of explicit communication. The parable, the fable, the bed time story are associated with relaxing, being comfortable, safe and familiar, but charged with messages.

Simile

Simile also has a role within therapy and pervades our daily life too, sometimes with therapy the connection needs spelling out, it needs to be more explicit. That is the nature of the simile, it is less subtle than the metaphor, the similarity between ideas and objects is clearly defined and spelled out, but it still utilises imaginative picturesque language that resonates with a client, there are times when this can still provide a powerful boost to understanding beyond the more basic statement of fact. Here are some examples of simile in daily use:

- As high as a kite
- As fit as a fiddle
- Like a bear with a sore head
- Clean as a whistle
- Busy as a bee
- Cool as a cucumber

As a therapist we are looking for that moment in the subconscious mind, when the message of the story clicks into place for the client, whether that be within psychotherapy or hypnotherapy.

Language is our tool, so we have the story we want to use, that connecting message, but how we deliver that message is important too, poetic rhythmic language gives us the smooth delivery we want. Many therapists use poems within their work and our metaphors can be poetic and powerful.

Why is poetic language powerful?

If our stories have rhythm and meter, we weave patterns that soothe the mind, like a lullaby for the mind, it helps to relax and then to deliver that message, the important message that the client's mind says, "you understand me", you have rapport. Understanding, connecting, rapport is where is starts, where our work starts and how we weave our words, or weave in the words of others into our words, helps us make that connection, that break through.

Poetry has the power of melody which is in itself trance inducing, it is like a musical piece and that musical piece creates and is harmony. Also at some deep level if something rhymes it gives you the feeling it must be true.

Dr Berry, formerly Fellow and Director of Studies in English at King's College, Cambridge, states that "Poetry is a powerful medium which can talk to our soul: "The best poetry takes us beyond the limitations of the rational mind. In antiquity the Greeks and Romans recognised that the mind had two main faculties or levels, and by the middle ages there was a firm distinction being made between *ratio* or reason, and the *intellectus*, the higher mind, which obtains knowledge through intuitive or direct apprehension (the *intellectus* was sometimes called *nous* by the Greeks). It is through this higher mind that Truth is apprehended. Poetry can take us into ways of saying and being closely allied to this intuitive state of knowing; they are beyond ordinary reason, but not irrational. So while in day to day life we are usually cut off from this level of experience, poetry and poetic language reunite us with it. The best poetry can lead us via abstract forms towards higher truths."

Let us look at one of the metaphors in this book to understand how and why it works, it is set out here like a poem rather than a script to emphasise its poetic nature, it is used to treat depression:

for most of us it feels stuck,
stuck in a place we cannot see out of
the bottom of a hole........
I am at the bottom of a hole
I cannot even be bothered to look and see if a ladder is there
If there is one it will probably be too short
Whatever I do, it just comes to nought
or that is how it feels
there is no way out
do not pass go
do not collect two hundred pounds
I am sapped and I am drained
with all the juice squeezed out
Like the juice of a battery, flat, just flat
do you feel like that sometimes? 0 power
You can plug in that battery and you can re-charge it
just a flicker at first of course
a flicker of life that builds and surges
and that life force re-emerges
if the battery of you car goes flat
get some jump leads
you can use those leads to spark your engine alive
that engine sparking with power
Yes, and you know you can survive,
keep that engine running for a while
take it for a spin and it is back on the road again
you are back on the road again........today,feeling that spark,
just a glimmer at first, but back on the road again

In this piece we are engaging with the client to get that feeling of being understood, we are using several interwoven metaphors to achieve this. We start with the idea of being stuck, "at the bottom of a hole" feeling trapped, then we move on to the lethargy of

5

ession, through not feeling able to even look to see if there is a way out of the hole, then we show the emptiness that comes with depression with the orange having it's juice all squeezed out, we then link into "juice" as power and the flat battery image, all this works together to this create the "you know what I feel" moment for the client, they are not alone in their experience of depression, your imagery makes them feel completely understood. However, we build out of the metaphor a message of hope, once we have created the connection with the client, we give the spark of life, through recharging the battery, building a metaphor of hope.

We as the therapists are helping to deliver that spark of hope to our clients, we even weave ourselves into the metaphor as the jump lead sparking the client back into life. The banal commonality of the image of sparking a car back into life is so very familiar to the client it can reach out to anyone. The metaphor works as a journey of metaphors to engage the client and then provides a solution to which the subconscious can relate. The use of repetition, rhyme and picturesque language helps soothe and lull the client into cooperation and engagement and bypasses resistance.

Metaphors in images

Visual images can be metaphors that can speak to our clients, you can then use this on a subliminal level, or perhaps more overtly. Selecting the images that you have on the walls of your work space to re-enforce the metaphors you use and then describing the images within hypnosis, can enhance the therapeutic experience, additionally getting the client to focus on the relevant image as part of the induction, will help the image to stay with them. An example from within the book is the metaphor of the sycamore seed, that is used primarily to assist people come to terms with adoption issues, but can be adapted to people making new beginnings and laying down new roots, a simple image of a sycamore seed or other seeds upon the wall will help to reinforce the message. In some instances it might be appropriate to give the client a copy of an image to focus on in meditation, or simply have on the wall at home to keep the idea live in their mind.

The cover of this book shows an image of a bicycle partially submerged in the water following some flooding. We can read something powerful here, the bike is to most people something they treasure, it becomes a part of them and riding someone else's bike is just not the same experience. There are other associations attached to the bicycle, it is more than just a mode of transport, it is a symbol of freedom too. In the image, this treasured belonging is submerged in water, this can symbolise loss, something feeling tainted or damaged or even freedom curtailed, but though the bike is submerged in flood water, this water will recede, the trouble will pass, the bike can be reclaimed again, polished and cared for and reunited with its owner, it is in fact a symbol of hope rather than destruction, a symbol of surviving the storms of life, the bike is not swept away, it is not lost forever, it is to be reclaimed, just as life can be reclaimed and freedom can return.

Within this book there are a wide range of metaphors created with poetic language to assist the therapist in their targeted communication with the client. The book is broken down into areas of treatment to make it easy to use, though some of the ideas can be used within alternative areas of treatment, some ideas for which are outlined following the script in italics. Sometimes it is just a fragment of an idea that is needed to create that understanding within the subconscious mind of the client, sometimes it needs a more detailed script. You may wish to create your own scripts from the kernel of an idea within the book. The metaphors presented can help you weave into your own words ideas that can enrich and stimulate your treatment plan for the client and lead to effective change.

Metaphors in Hypnosis

The metaphors presented in this book do not have to be used in hypnosis and increasingly psychotherapists use metaphors and poems in their work. However the metaphor is at the heart of the work of hypnotherapy and being in trance can assist delivering the message home to the client. The success of this message depends on how comfortable the client is with the idea of trance and how you explain this to them may impact on the efficacy of your treatment. Too many television programmes exist showing people doing ridiculous things under hypnosis for a degree of wariness if not fear to now be hovering somewhere in the clients psyche.

The Trance State

Taking time to explain to the client is worthwhile as it is empowering for them, to be asked to relax in front of a complete stranger who does not explain what you are going to experience and how it might feel is an unrealistic expectation. An explanation you can use with a client follows: a trance state is something each of us experiences everyday; it is a completely natural state one that happens at least twice a day. When you first wake up in the morning and you have not opened your eyes yet, you are just becoming conscious, you are aware of sound, such as perhaps birds singing outside but cannot quite bring yourself to open your eyes yet, you feel cosy and comfortable and unaffected by troubles and demands of your daily life, this is a trance state. When you are just drifting off to sleep at night, we feel the same, drowsy and comfortable we are still slightly conscious but unaffected by an active mind, this is a trance state.

We also drift into a trance state at different times during the day, less deep perhaps but nonetheless a trance state. For example; when you have driven along the motorway and you suddenly realise that you have passed junction turn offs and had not noticed; you have finished all the washing up but do not remember doing it ; when you are playing an instrument and it feels like the instrument is almost playing itself, you become so focused and that the outside world disappears; when you are doing something creative like painting or maybe even something active like dancing or repetitive exercise, in all these situations we can zone out and drift into a trance state. There is a kind of music labelled as trance, one that is repetitive and lulls you into a zone where nothing outside the experience matters and maybe this concept can help understand the trance.

We are either fully awake, in the drowsy in-between state or asleep. We are not looking within hypnosis to become fully unconscious, it is not about being "knocked out", sometimes people use the expression being "put under", but you are not going under anything, if you lose all conscious awareness you have simply fallen asleep, or drifted into a light doze, there are no hidden other places for your mind to go. In this state your brain waves slow down into what is known as the alpha state, beta is alert, alpha is drowsy, calm, we reach this state when meditating or doing something creative, it is just a case of slowing down the mind. Following this are the theta and delta states when the brain waves have slowed down enough to allow sleep to occur.

In hypnotherapy we are coaching people into a trance state for a therapeutic purpose. When someone is in the trance state we can access their subconscious mind and affect changes in behaviour. When in a trance the conscious mind has gone partly off duty, it is there but not in controlling mode. This is the only way we can access the subconscious to affect a change, it is like the hard drive on your computer with a faulty programme that we need to work on and repair, or to use an older metaphor it is a pre-recorded tape that needs recording over. This can also be achieved through self hypnosis, if you have the will to make a change then hypnosis can open the door to that change.

Metaphors for Therapy:
Addictions

When we are working in the area of addiction, we are looking for ways to break the pattern of the addiction, once the pattern is broken, then sustaining the break becomes easier.

Sugar addiction – Tidal Wave

So what is it about sugar.......refined sugar that is.....the word refined is interesting, makes it sound elegant.....something special...... but of course it is not.........like so many things being sold to us that we do not need........ it pops up everywhere......not just in cakes and chocolate and biscuits......but hidden away in cereals and sauces..... we get hooked.....just like a drug and then we think we need it, so many people think they need it for energy......just sold the idea by the people who want to make money out of you needing that fix......or thinking you need that fix.....it is no good for us....poisons our body.....now we know these days that smoking is bad for us, even though years ago it was sold to us to help with breathing diseases, they sold that for health once too.......we know not to drink too much alcohol....but do we know why? Too much sugar.....bad for the liver as the liver cannot process so much sugar....so what about the cakes and the biscuits and the chocolate.....the sugar turns to fat, well you may not mind that.....you may not mind the fat clinging to your cells......but what else is happening that we just cannot see..... going on inside our body as it gets overwhelmed by the sugar.....a surging tidal wave of sugar.....a tsunami of sugar

I do not want to sound like an extremist or anything about this sugar problem, but I am sure you have heard about people with diabetes being at the risk of going blind, that is because too much sugar is toxic........the body has reached the point that it cannot process it any more........

We have to produce so much insulin to combat the sugar in our body that it affects the circulation, the arteries.....they just cannot cope.....overwhelmed......drowning in the stuff.....one study actually says that sugar stimulates cancer cells.....and this stuff is hidden in the foods we buy in the supermarket......a hidden toxin.....they bang on and on about smoking.....they have banned it in public places so you do not have to take it in without a choice, what about a warning on our biscuits, our cereals..... that tomato sauce........this can seriously damage your health..... it can cause Alzheimer now they say.......did you know the half of it? I am just letting you know, just in case, I do not think they want us to know.......too much money to be made.....made from making us addicts.....duping us, but I want to say no to all this sugar.....I want to protect those precious cells in my body, my liver, my heart, what about you?

Are you going to let them make money out of making you a sugar addict.....people stop smoking.....drinking...... heroin too.......so how about this sugar thing, how about stopping that flooding of your body with that sugar

Imagine for me the beautiful rolling countryside out there, green fields, lush healthy grass, trees standing tall, sheep or is it cows grazing, I do not know it is your field, there may even be horses there.......some tender plants along some hedgerows perhaps, I love the sight of poppies swaying in a gentle breeze, their wonderful vibrant natural colour bursting out from amongst grasses or maybe ripe buds of corn, cornflowers blue, all the beauty of our countryside ....out there and then that tidal wave arrives a tsunami of sugary substance.....of sticky gooey...... cloying sugar, a wave of a glutinous sugary gloop just drowning it and sweeping everything away with it.........destroying that beauty out there.....like a disaster movie......destroying the natural world, destroying all in it's path this wave of sugary gloop, I just wanted you to imagine it that way.......it might be easier than seeing it flooding your body, creating devastation in your body........ sticking to the cells so they cannot work properly.......clogging things up....... I thought you might be able to see that better, a metaphor for your body......but you can of course imagine your body under siege from the sugar.........overwhelmed.......cells damaged ....your body trying to pump it out, get rid of it........ it is not holding that wave of sugar........ but you can stop this destruction..........you can save yourself........now you know just what it can do....now you know just how bad it is for you......you can just say no and if you see those biscuits or sweets in the shops.....you will see a heath warning on it, a poison, toxic sign and nothing and no one, will make you pick it up, or eat it, no one and nothing will make you do that........I know that now and you know it too, taking care of you now.......in fact I wonder when you will realise that you do not notice those sweet foods any more.......they are no longer a part of your life, no need to think about it anymore, because you have taken control, I know now you get it, now you know what to do.........not doing this now is not an option open to you, no longer seeing those foods as foods............after all there is no nutrition there in those cakes and biscuits.........nothing you need in there and you eat for nourishment to nourish your body and I know that is what you do now.

Alternative uses for this script:

The sugar addiction script can be used to assist in the treatment of alcohol addiction, the effect of the sugar in alcohol can often be overlooked, alcoholics can go on to develop diabetes, focusing on this awareness can be a useful addition to the treatment plan.

Smoking cessation – Poisons

Now I do not know about you but I think that stale smell of cigarettes is a pretty bad smell.... a smell that clings to your clothes....... lingers in a room....... sticks to your breath....... a rather horrible smell....... now smell is an important thing for us humans.......our sense of smell is there to warn us of danger....... like the smell of rotting fish.....or rotten eggs.....the smell of burning rubber.....a smell to let us know that something is wrong.......that it is something to be avoided.......so what is your nose telling you.......those cigarettes are bad for you.....full of toxins.....poisons which you are breathing in...... now air is your primary energy source, you need air more than you need water or food.......the air comes first......so why would you poison it before you breathe it in, there is arsenic in that cigarette.....a poison.....would you eat a meal laced with arsenic? Would you drink a drink laced with arsenic? I mean it is up to you of course....... but I would be surprised if you would decide to deliberately go for the arsenic.......you need that fresh clean air to live, so you can turn over a new leaf now....a new page and this clean white fresh page, you can start your story again..... leaving the smoking thing behind you in the past and what of the future, what about your life in the future.

I would like you to imagine yourself a year from now......you have not been smoking for a whole year..... I wonder what he/she would say to you about the decision you have made today....... I wonder what they would say about making this change......." thank you", I am sure would be up there amongst the things they would say..... I feel so much fitter..... healthier, perhaps that too, I can smell things...... I can smell the salty sea air again or a freshly cut lawn.........I can taste my food so much better because I can smell it, I wonder what else they might say............I can make it up the stairs without panting now..... I am training for the marathon.......I have taken up a sport.......or perhaps I just feel good about myself.........I feel good that I made a decision and I stuck to it, something I did for me, taking care of me now....... I wonder if you can think of anything else they might say to you........ this you a year down the line, I will just let you think for a bit......

Cocaine addiction – Choose a Door

I would like you to imagine you are in a big country house and walking up an ornate staircase at the top............at the top of the stairs........ is a selection of doors...........these doors lead into your future......your future five years from now..........but there are choices that you make now that will influence that future......... the door to your left is the one where you have carried on taking coke...... and the door to the right is the one where you gave it up today and have been clean for five years.

Let us take a look through the left hand door........ take a look at your life.......What does your skin look like? ....How is your nose holding up? Your teeth? ....sorry to be so direct but you need to look at this............ Do you have a loving partner or have a series of people given up on you? ....Do you have a job? ....What do your family think of you? Do you have any family? How is the debt situation? ....What sort of home can you afford?.............

Now let's close that door, let's turn our backs on that option and look through the other door, What do you look like? ....you have been clean for five years........... friends around you............. a loving partner and family that is proud of you...........there with you..........who are proud of you........ obviously which you choose is up to you...........but know and understand you are making a choice now.......... you are choosing your future......... you are choosing your life....Which doorway do you want to choose........now you know you have a choice.....

Alternative uses for this script.

Alcohol addiction: the basis of this script can be adapted to alcoholism, removing references to the nose and teeth, but emphasising the effects of alcohol on the liver, adding all the effects on the body from alcohol and working with the impact on family life, known references to the client's specific situation can be included, such as "do you still see your children? What do they think of you?"

Gambling: if the physical impact of the addiction is removed from this script and an emphasis placed on the financial losses and the lifestyle changes, this can be powerful for gamblers, one can also add specific personal references to make it more real when the client visualises the future.

Gambling – The Con Man

You work hard for the money in your pocket......I wonder why you would just throw it away, I mean, I can understand giving it to a good cause.......a deserving cause like a charity but some faceless money man exploiting others....... paying towards yet another car for them or a luxury jet......you might as well set fire to it, watch it burn as let them steal it from you...... cheating you of your hard earned money.....how do you feel I wonder about them cheating you of your money? Are you angry at them for cheating you? Surely you are not going to let them do it again, are you?

I wonder what you stand to lose..... no one likes to lose..... gamblers always lose the odds are stacked against them, the way to win is not to give them your money...... after all it makes you feel so bad when you realise what you have lost, you can not get that back but you can stop them cheating you again and again...... it is like running into a brick wall and knowing it will hurt but doing it just the same.....why would you choose to do something that hurts you? the gambling hurts you and not just you, others around you, people you love.........I know you would do so much to protect those you love, you are that kind of person.......you would want to protect them, this not gambling is such a small thing to do for them when you think of all that you would do if you could do it for them.......... I think you know now how to stop them cheating you.......the anonymous faces behind the machines and the computer screens........

I wonder how long it took for you to earn the money they took from you last time.......what time you had to put into earning it before they took it from you, you can choose now not to let them do it to you anymore, you can choose to protect yourself from their greed for your money........ I think you will choose now not to do it....... I think you know that now too, of course your conscious mind knew all along what they were up to, setting traps for you........ making it so easy to lose it, but now your unconscious mind knows it too, it will help you now, so this gambling thing is in the past, a past chapter of your life.........in this chapter....... the chapter unfolding now has no gambling in it..........nor the next, nor the one after that, in fact you will find that it is left in the past where it belongs, along with other things that no longer have any part of your life and you can see yourself in the future now.......way into the future, knowing what to do to prevent that loss to gambling.......you know now......you are in charge of what you do and you would not deliberately choose to lose, that person is in the past.....I wonder what you will do will all that money that you do not lose any more, what can you do for you now?

Relapse – Snakes and Ladders

I wonder if you ever played snakes and ladders as a child....or maybe you have played it as an adult.......just to remind you about snakes and ladders.....it involves a collection of numbered squares.....from 1 to 100....the squares are often colourful.....1 is at the bottom and 100 is at the top.......now you probably remember......I guess you remember that the aim of the game is to get from 1 to 100...........you throw a dice and you move the number of squares that you are given......then up and up you go.....I wonder if you remember that unstoppable determination of childhood to get to the top.......to be the first to get to the top.......to win the game......you can be helped along the way by landing on a square with a picture of a ladder.........this helps you skip up a couple of rows as you go nearer and nearer the top...... but of course it can go the other way round......you can land on the image of the snake and you slide down again.........but one of the things to remember is........that even if you hit one of the snake squares.......you never go all the way back to the beginning........the game is not totally lost....totally over......you are still in with a chance....you need to pick yourself up again..... and start making your way back up again and you never know, there could be another ladder......another ladder there to springboard you back towards the top.......so if just your subconscious is listening right now......it get's what I am saying.......but maybe your conscious mind needs a bit of help.......so you have been doing really well.....sober for so long and you have had a blip........a slip.......a relapse........you have slipped back down again......but the game is not over.......you are not back to where you started........you can get back on track again......I know you can get back on track again and start heading towards the 100........your goal......to be free of alcohol for good now........so get back to it now......working at it now......with that same determination now.....the determination to win now........I know you can do it.....because I have seen how determined you are......and I have seen just what other people can do too......when they put their mind to it.....focus in and begin to take control again........no more alcohol.......you are back on track again....... You are not back at the beginning now.....you have made good progress.......heading back towards the top again........

Alternative uses for this script:

This script can obviously be used for any kind of addiction, including over-eating and snacking, or any kind of habitual behaviour. The aim is to prevent the client feeling hopeless for having a lapse and using the lapse to give up trying to change altogether. The script can be adapted to any situation where the client is trying to affect change and sometimes struggling with that, even a relationship break-down where they feel the need to keep contacting the ex-partner. It can sometimes be helpful to give the client a picture of a snakes and ladders board to reinforce the message of the metaphor and give them a sense of what they are aiming to achieve. You can assign a number of squares they can go up the board each sober week, to give them a sense of progress, with the aim of reaching the top and not needing the addiction any more, not needing your support any more. They can keep the image afterwards as a reminder of their achievement and to keep them on track.

Anger

Anger – Short Fuse

Sometimes people use the expression having a short fuse......I wonder what your fuse is like....is it long?.....or perhaps it is short?.....or maybe it has been in the past?.....someone just says.......or maybe does the wrong thing....or it feels wrong to you......then "bam"....off you go.........but it never feels very good afterwards does it?...... "bam" and then there is carnage everywhere........ people upset....drama all around......but it is just this fuse thing.....how do we stop the short fuse?....or maybe make the fuse a little longer to give you time to think....time to decide how you really feel.............well you know there is a way......just imagining that fuse in your mind for a moment..... there is a big barrel of gunpowder like in an old film or a cartoon perhaps.....so you have the keg of gun powder there and a trail of powder leading away from it......I wonder if you can see it in your mind?.........and there is fire blazing a trail along the powder towards the keg ....I wonder if you can see it?......see it fizzing along......if you were there watching this and you wanted it to stop.......wanted to stop that huge explosion, what would you do? ....how about chucking some water onto it......or smothering it with a fire blanket........or even stamping on it with a heavy boot........there is always a way to damp out the spark...... muffle it.....drown it and stop it.........if you feel that spark flaring........just stop for a moment......you have got some time........even with a short fuse, for that fuse to be stopped.... interrupted......halted.....even just a second or two and you can stop the explosion.....hit the pause button and stop or even rewind.....rewind to a place before it began and see things in a new more comfortable light....your subconscious mind is just waiting for the signal, to know it can stop, so you can stop it now, can you not...whenever you want to you can stop.......

Anxiety

Anxiety becomes a conditioned response in certain situations and is governed by a sense of being out of control, so effective treatment requires breaking that conditioning and giving a sense of control back to the client, the metaphors presented here have been designed to do just that.

Breaking conditioning – Elephants

In India when an elephant is very small.... they tie a rope around it's leg and tie it to a tree..... the baby elephant pulls and it tugs.... it pulls and it tugs to try to break free...... until it is too tired to pull any more......... it gives in....tired and exhausted.... it believes it is trapped by the rope forever.........

When that elephant is fully grown....and if tied to that tree could pull it right down........to control the elephant.....that powerful majestic animal....... they just have to tie a rope around its leg.........it stands still........ it believes it cannot go anywhere........ because of its experience as a baby elephant......... it could actually roam wherever it wanted to................. but just the feeling of the rope around its leg has conditioned it............. conditioned it into thinking it is trapped............ but it is actually trapped by the memory........... trapped by a thought................. all it needs to do is break free from that conditioning and it could do what it wants.............. now I know you understand more than that elephant................. I know that you know................ just because something has happened once in your life that it does not mean it will happen again................I know you will keep trying................ keep testing the boundaries................ so that you are not trapped by what happened before................ held captive but what was and may never be again............ breaking free................. breaking free of your boundaries and going where you want............. trying what you want.............. finding your own way.............. not trapped by a thought. Imaginary bonds cannot tie you.............. tie you to the past like that poor elephant............. that powerful majestic elephant............. standing sadly.......... looking at all the trees in the distance................ wanting to explore wanting to roam.......... but standing there, with a rope around its leg............. tied to nothing...........tied to nothing at all............. you will break free and go where you will.

Taming the mind – Wild Horses

The sages of India describe the thoughts in the mind like wild horses....... wild horses thundering across a sandy beach....... chasing through the waters...... the spray rising up as they gallop through the water...... wild...... unleashed..... untamed..... racing along....... those thoughts chasing along....... chasing along the beach........ wild thoughts...... chasing wildly one after another...... powerful muscles....... powering along the beach....... take control of those horses....... slow them down............ a gallop to a canter.......... watch them slowing down as they move across the beach............ a canter to a trot............. trotting more gently.......... trotting along the beach........... those thoughts calming........ less wild, calming down............ thoughts slowing down............. a trot to a walk now............. the horse slowed down now to a walk............. a sedate walk along the beach........... thoughts slowing now........... slowing right down now........... the horses stop............. come to a standstill.................... those wild horses..........tamed, stilled........... standing still on the beach.......... chests heaving as they rest and recuperate............. resting still..........calming........... calming and resting............. thoughts still now.......... so still now and calm............. thoughts slowed to a standstill.............. like those wild horses tamed.............. slowed, calmed.......... calm thoughts now........... so still.............a still calm mind now............. now you can bring those horses to a standstill.......... calming them, soothing them............. like a horse whisperer.............a horse whisperer who can calm the horses................. calm thoughts................. so relaxed and still now.

Taking Control – Television

You can take control back, take control of your thoughts........... just as you can choose the channel on your television.............. where have the controls gone?.......... did someone walk off with the control............ are they in their back pocket?........... in another room?.......... on the kitchen table or perhaps they have fallen down the back of the sofa?.............. I wonder where the controls are? You can find them................. find the controls or take them back from someone who may have taken them............. get hold of those controls................ feel them in your hands............ all the buttons to press.............. I wonder what colours they are?............ how the controls feel in your hands again?................ so good to have the controls back and be able to choose again................. you can choose calm comfortable thoughts.............. or you can choose the scary thoughts............. the scary channel........... the channel that has frightened you........... or the channel which only has good news.......... good thoughts........... calm and happy thoughts..........now you have the controls back............ back in your hands........... I think you will choose the calm thoughts.............. turning off the scary ones............. someone else left that on, you are in control now............. you can chose........... take control...........take control of the controls and allow yourself to feel good........... feeling warm........... comfortable thoughts wash over you........ pressing the button.......... that's right...........so good it feels to be back in control.

Trains as Thoughts

I like to think of the mind like a station........a busy station with trains coming in from all directions......the trains represent our thoughts.......so many thoughts coming and going....going and coming.....now if your busy mind were a station........just imagine

21

all the trains coming and going......and now imagine ....
if you were at the station waiting for a train.....would you board
the first train that arrived......the first to pull up to the platform.....
or would you consider the journey you want to take.......the place
you want to go.......would you look at the board and check if
that is your train pulling in.........and only board the train you
need....or would you just jump on the first train that arrives.......
you can of course wait for that right train to arrive....you see
........we can board any train.........any train that arrives............
and end up at a random destination.......which might be fun at
times......but most of the time we have a specific destination.......
we do not want to waste time on a detour back to where we need
to be.....or even end up somewhere threatening and scary.....
somewhere out of bounds..........so just thinking about this
station....coming back to this station that is our mind.......start
thinking about the trains that you board......start taking control
and not just jumping aboard.....think about where you want to
go.....and choose the route you want....reject the random
thoughts....the thoughts that might scare you.........or divert
you.......take you down dead ends.........end of the line kind of
thoughts.........find the thought you want......that will take you
where you want to go........

Choice – Focus

When you stand upon a beach you can choose to let your eyes
take in the whole scene around you.........or you can adjust your
eyes.............like looking through a pair of binoculars...... do
you want to look at the surf, as the tide rolls in and out..........
the waves unfurling and withdrawing....................if that
absorbs your attention, you will not be noticing the seagull that
twists and twirls above your head, even though he emits a piercing
call..........or will you look out to the horizon.............that hard
blue line where sky and sea meet.................will that absorb
your focus.................your attention.............or perhaps a
boat cutting through the water...........maybe that will take your
attention......... foam spray flying up at its bows and seagulls

22

clustered, whirling low over the deck in case of a chance to steal from the catch...........you can choose to focus on any of these things.............or the pebbles beneath you...................the different colours and shapes perhaps feeling the texture in your fingertips...............the choices are yours.............what you choose to give your attention......

When you are at a concert....................perhaps a rock concert........... you hear the whole sound........... carried by the sound.................feeling it pulse through your body.......... but you can also choose to focus within the sound................... breaking the sound down and focusing on the lead guitar and the rest of the sound steps back a little.............or you can focus on the drums...................that rhythmic intense beat............. following it closely or the accompanying bass guitar................ you can choose to let the whole sound pulse through you or give one instrument more of your attention............. more choices that come your way and if you are standing to hear this concert are you aware of how long you have been standing.............are you moving to the music..............do you do this instinctively or are you aware of each small movement, as each foot is lifted in turn.............your arms perhaps moving at your side, or swaying in the air ....when you are clapping, do you notice the slight sharp discomfort as they meet or are you so engrossed in the sound you do not notice that small discomfort....

We have a choice upon which we focus............I wonder if you have had the experience of having a headache.......................or a pain somewhere and the phone rings and you have a really interesting conversation and for a while all awareness of that headache goes away..........it is only after you put the phone down and probe around and search for that awareness of the headache ....you search for it ....then you begin to notice it again, what we give our attention to grows .... and becomes dominant.............whether it is a thought or a feeling.............you can feed the pain................ fan the flames of it by giving it all of your attention.......................or you can

starve it of your attention like starving a fire of oxygen...........
whether it is a thought....a feeling....an awareness....a sensation...
you can choose...it is up to you...there is a Native American
Indian story that you may have heard... it is one of those
apocryphal stories where a grandfather is teaching his grandson
about life, he tells his grandson that there is a fight between two
wolves going on inside him, one was unhappy and troubled the
other contented and peaceful, when asked which wolf will win the
fight, the grandfather says it will be the wolf that he feeds..........
So....Choose carefully what you feed in your mind, the ideas that
you feed with your attention and focus your awareness...it is
entirely up to you, no one else but you....

Alternative uses for this script:

*This script focusing on choice has many applications as in so
many treatment areas choice is a factor, such as addictions and
habits, the choice to focus on recovery from illness, the choice to
fight back in an abusive relationship, the choice to make change in
any area of life.*

Cancer

Cancer – Gardening

You are going into a garden in a moment....it is a very special garden...it is your garden and no one else can come here....it is walled in and protected....you have not been here for a while.... you have not visited the garden.....you have opened the gate and stepped in and find to your surprise that Chinese bindweed...that pest of a weed...has somehow got into the garden...your special garden....it is choking some of your most beautiful plants and shrubs...hampering their growth...choking them....but you know exactly what you need to do....what you need to do to save your garden...to protect your lovely plants...those plants that have been relying on you for protection...first you need to cut the bind weed back...hefting your shears and cutting it down....see yourself cutting it down.......cutting it right back so you can see the plants underneath now...that had been struggling to get nourishment from the sun....as the weed had been blocking the light...they can get their nourishment from the sun now and begin to thrive again...that bind weed has been stealing their water too...taking all the water that has soaked into the soil...thus starving the plants even more of the nourishment that they needed...but you can deal with that too... you have chopped back all the visible weed now....but you need to get down into the soil and root out the roots....the damaging roots of the weeds....getting your trowel and digging out the roots....digging them all out....not letting one tiny root escape your attention...see yourself digging out the roots........working hard.....rooting out all the weeds...the damaging weeds....clearing the ground...freeing your plants from the damaging weeds...drying our those weeds...so that you can burn them....destroy them....getting rid of that damaging weed... pulling it up....drying it out....and creating a wonderful bonfire of it....destroying it once and for all....

You can do this now...you have all the strength and ability to root it all out and destroy it....working hard...being rewarded for that work as you see the garden return to its previous beauty...well nourished...thriving....healthy...taking all the weeds you have cut down and the roots you have dug out of the soil and creating a huge bonfire....destroying all the weeds...not one single damaged cell surviving...weeded out...destroyed....gone....it cannot spread any more as every last trace of it has gone. ..feeling stronger... healthier....surveying your beautiful garden now....fully recovered...seeing it in full bloom....the green of the well-tended lawn....the colours of the shrubs and flowers...all the beautiful colours of nature all around you...a garden in full bloom... magnificent...and you can rest on a bench now....your work done....your work complete....but keeping a vigilant eye now.... for any sign of a weed...that might damage your wonderful garden....policing it well...protecting it....protecting your garden...your own special place...and your subconscious mind.... understands the stories that I tell....and works hard to protect you...destroying those cancer cells...weeded out and destroyed... every last cancer cell weeded out and destroyed.....leaving you strong and well-nourished and well cared for.

Immune system for cancer – The Armoury

You have missiles in your armoury to fight those rogue cells..... like those heat sensing drones we hear so much about.....your killer K cells seek out those rogue cells..... hunt them down..... seek them out, follow them until they can blast them.....destroy them.....seeking them out............until they find every last one....... destroying them and then they leave your system..... processed through like the debris they are.....unwanted...... un-needed. ....

So you go the toilet, you are peeing them out of your body, those waste cells.......drinking plenty of fluids and flushing them out..... broken.....beaten rogue cells leaving your body.......as that drone patrols your system.....seeking..... ever seeking those rogue cells and destroying them on 24 hour watch.......always on watch..... looking out.....surveying your system...hunting them down...then you let them go...waste product...not wanted...letting go....

Confidence

Confidence – Modelling – My Story

I know what it is like to be worried and scared not knowing how to do something right...........will you get it right?....... how did I get myself into this situation anyway?......I want to go home.......I don't want this you know......when I was young I got a job at The Sunday Times....... not sure how I got there........talked my way in and one day I looked around at all these smart people.......these dynamic people and thought how can I keep up with them?........ what will I do?....... maybe they will realise I am a fraud.......out of my depth and not waving but drowning as that old poem said......... I looked around the office and saw a woman I thought was the best, so confident she was.......smart and clever........one day I watched her give a presentation to our boss.......she was brilliant..... I thought.......that is how I want to be.......who I want to be I thought........so I watched and I learned.....what did she do that was so special?......how did she stand?.......how did she talk?.......move her hands.....use her voice........what did she say?.......what made her so good at what she did?........I kept watching and learning and then practising........I copied her style, I became an actress, a mimic........I was going to be her.......one day my moment came.........my big presentation to the boss.......I was a little worried of course but in some ways not........because it was not me doing the presentation.......it was her, I was going to be just like her.....it went down a storm and I felt really good being her, it came easily, fluidly, I got all the words right, said them just right.......I was a success and it got easier each time.....in a year I was promoted.......in a year later, yet again........I stopped thinking about how and what to do.......I no longer had to think about how to speak and how to stand........then one day a new girl started on the team and I saw her watching me, a couple of months on and her moment came.......her big presentation to the

28

boss and guess what? as I watched her I realised, that was me! She was talking and standing and using her hands just like me........it was I now who was the example of what to do......I could not believe it, what is it they say? imitation is the sincerest form of flattery....... well I do not know about that.......all I know is that if I ever feel out of my depth now and want to do something new......I find the expert and just do what they do!

Negative self talk – Tuning out

As you relax there I want to ask you a question........ you do not need to answer this question out loud...... just thinking about it......processing it in your mind.........deep in your subconscious mind.......I was just wondering if you ever talk to yourself in your head....... most of us do, you know........but how often is that voice an encouraging one.......how often does it say well done? Does it tell you off? Attack you and chide you? I wonder what it is that you say to you?.......critical and hurtful, encouraging and loving........which is it to be? Has it been.........will it be........I wonder?.......I sometimes wonder if your harshest critic is you and if someone else spoke to you like that, just what would you do? ....Would you argue with them? ....Tell them off? ....Or would you just let it be? I am wondering all this as you lie there now............ peacefully wondering perhaps why you let that voice in.......that negative one.......the critical one.

You could always turn the volume down I guess......you have the controls to turning that voice down......... the one that attacks and chides you and choose a different channel, tuning in to a different thought.......perhaps looking for and finding something that you know you did well........ that you can pat yourself on the back for and say well done.........it is hard in our culture sometimes, I know we are discouraged from saying the things we are good at and playing it down in that self depreciating way..........but everyone is good at something and it is ok........at least allow that voice in your head to say it......no one else is listening .....it is ok!

If you heard something on the radio you just could not stand, a song that you loathe perhaps..........you can get up and change the channel.......you can tune right in, to something that you like.......something that makes you feel good as you swivel that dial........different sounds echoing through until you find that station you want, like getting off at the right station.......in the car perhaps........at the place you want to be, or is that radio, old fashioned now, a thing of the past.......what about the TV then, choosing the channel there........not the one that you hate....... you would not make yourself sit.....hour after hour watching and listening,....listening and watching something you cannot stand when there is an alternative choice.......so many channels to choose from now.......it is up to you.......you have the power, the choice, you can turn off that voice.......that hurtful one in your head.......perhaps as you lie there in your bed and review things past or those that are yet to come.....bring the cheerleaders, cheering you on.....that is the choice that you have and I wonder which one you will choose now?......You can switch it off and make it stop, that negative voice, turn it off, make it stop and you can, can you not????

Finding confidence – Bubbles

Your subconscious mind has all that you need to bring happiness into your life.......... deep down in the depths of your subconscious............ like a deep sea....your subconscious mind with fathomless depths............. allow the feelings locked deep down in those depths............... memories that have brought you happiness............. experiences that have brought you pleasure..... they may be buried deep...... deep down........... allow them to bubble up to the surface like bubbles surface upon the water.......... popping into the air............small bubbles at first............ small feelings of joy............. allow them to the surface and make them bigger............... Stronger............... good feelings surfacing............. bubbling to the surface from deep down below.......... lost at the bottom of your subconscious for some time perhaps but allowing them up now.

At first it may feel like those good feelings are just out of your reach............... it may feel like a glimmer in your peripheral vision.......... something there but not quite there, glimmering there..........just at the edge of your sight............. allowing it to come into focus......... allowing yourself to see those good feelings that have bubbled up to the surface.......... feel them come clearly into sight.......... see them clearly, making that feeling stronger............. sharper...........clearer............. those good feelings can be there now.......... allowing them back in. So strong now. ....feeling it............. remembering how it feels to feel good.............making it stronger.......... and those bubbles increasing now as you allow them up to the surface................

You begin to notice those feelings more and more as the days pass.

It may have started slowly at first but now, now you notice those moments of pleasure in your daily life............. those feelings that you had been overlooking.......... but will not overlook anymore........... you may wonder why you had overlooked these good feelings in the past, but you will not overlook them anymore......... so good, strong and powerful......... as you begin to notice those good feelings they become ever stronger.......... more powerful........ choosing positive thoughts............. it is in your power to choose now and why would you want to suppress those good thoughts............ no longer burying them deep, allowing them up and enjoying them............ and this is not something that you will not find easy now.......... That's right.

Limiting yourself – Believing a False Story

I think we have talked about the stories we create in our heads...... the story that limits us........the story of who we are and what we are capable of.......we define ourselves through our family.... where we were born....our education.....our gender....we create an image of ourselves.....then we add in experiences....experiences that we think define us....but they can limit us too....an experience can change us and limit us....and give us a story that we tell ourselves day after day....so we believe it to be true...it becomes reality because we believe it....we do not test it.....we need to test those stories that we tell ourselves, that limit us....is it real?....how did I reach that conclusion?....is it based in fact?....let me tell you a story...it is one of the stories I told myself for a while....one day years ago I was asked to appear on camera and be interviewed....i enjoyed public speaking, so I thought it would be fun....I thought I would be good at it....everyone said I would.....I went on camera and I froze....I just could not get my words out.... my usually fluid speech just dried up....I was a disaster....I told myself this....I was a disaster on film and I just could not do it I said....from that day on, I said I was no good on camera....a couple of years passed and I was asked to do it again...I cannot do that, I said...I am just really bad at it....but I was told that I had to do it...I was really shaky and stressed because I had told myself for so long now, that I was bad on camera...I believed the story.... and so the story was true...it was awful again.....so from then on, I avoided all work on camera...got someone else to do it....and my story grew....then it became necessary for me to consider it again...for my work again...it was down to me and I began to question my story....I had been on camera twice in my whole life....I expected to be good first time and did not meet my own expectation and the story began...but who is brilliant at anything first time...when you ride a bicycle for the first time, you generally fall off....when we learn to write, we are not shakespeare overnight....we fall, when we learn to walk....we miss the goal, when we shoot a football....how had I created this massive story about how bad I was?....out of something I had done twice....I may never be the best on camera....like, not everyone can be David Beckham at football....but with a little practice, I could do it....I could try harder and work at getting it right....not giving up at the first hurdle....and so can you....learn from this story.... challenge your story...whatever your story is....whatever story, that you want to change.....do not limit yourself, by your story... write a new story...the one where you can change....you can learn and change just as you can learn from my story.....

Improving Self Image – The Mirror

As you continue to relax...I would like you to imagine there is a mirror in front of you....up on the wall in front of you...at just the right height for you.....perhaps an elaborate frame around the mirror...or is it plane....head and shoulders there in the mirror..... how often do you look in the mirror I wonder?....really look in the mirror....a quick brush of the hair...check the clothes look ok...make-up...shaving....do you really look?...if you do what do you see?....our family...our friends....our colleagues...they look at us all the time...they know our face better than we do...they know our expressions....our expressions the key to our feelings.... sometimes showing more than we know....look in that mirror and imagine what others see...how do they see us?....i wonder if they see you as you see you, or do they see you differently....i am sure you have seen mirrors in films...two way mirrors in films...where perhaps a suspect is being interviewed and watched from behind the mirror...so they can be observed....another behind that mirror....well the mirror you are looking at in your mind now...

That mirror has someone that loves you behind it...they are looking right at you...so what do they see...we tend to notice our imperfections....that is what we focus on....but what do they see...they see us differently...they see the good things...both inside and out...they see our good qualities...what do they think now as they look at you...imagine the thought they have...that lift of the spirits they feel when they see you...you know that feeling you have when you see someone you love in the street when they do not know you are looking....catching them not knowing they are observed...that unexpected feeling of love ad protection when you catch them unawares....the person that loves you has such feelings too....perhaps that is what they feel when they look at you through the mirror...thinking about the reasons they love you....perhaps leave love out of it...why do they like you....think about why they like you....what would they say now if whilst watching you someone asked them...what is good about you....in day to day life there is rarely time to do this, find out how they feel...sometimes we are inhibited to say how we feel...feel we are giving something away....giving our power away perhaps...but here it is safe...they can tell you what they like about you...respect about you....what draws them to you.....

I am going to be quiet for a few moments to allow you to absorb their positive words...allowing them to sink in....like water soaking into a sponge, their words sinking in... why they have drawn you into their life...and kept you there....now look at yourself with their words....why they like and respect you....see yourself through their eyes...their eyes on the other side of the mirror...see yourself now in a new light....you may want to do this thinking of different people who like you...as we have different relationships ....different people bring out different qualities within us...appreciate different strengths within us... allow yourself to know all that is good in you....allow yourself to see clearly in the mirror...to see yourself as you truly are...and not the distorted image we can build of ourselves...seeing all that is wrong...like one of those joke mirrors in the fairground...where everything is twisted and distorted...see you as you truly are.....so all that is good in you, I know that you can do this now, really looking now and seeing you.

Deepening

Staircase

I would like you to imagine you are standing at the top of a beautiful sweeping staircase, with a gentle curve as it bends and sweeps down into a large hallway........ the kind you see in a stately home....... perhaps it is made of marble.....or wood.....or even concrete......there are pictures on the walls to the side of you as you stand at the top of this staircase that will take you down........ down......... seeing the staircase before you now as you stand at the top......ready to make your way down....... as you make your way down the staircase I will be counting backwards from 10 to 1............. you may want to match your steps down to the numbers as I count........ starting with 10 and taking your fist step down....... beginning to allow yourself to relax......... now 9. .... just going a little deeper now as you start to progress down the staircase.............. 8....... seeing the lovely pictures on the walls as you go deeper down............ 7....... the staircase is beginning to curve as you make your way down deeper..........6....... each step down taking you deeper and deeper into a relaxing trance now......nothing to do now........5....... as you go down the staircase........I wonder if you can hear the sound you make as you take each step down 4........... so much more relaxed and comfortable now........3........ feeling that comfort spreading through you now as you go down the staircase 2........ you are nearly there now 1......... you are relaxed and comfortable....so deep now.

Counting

I suppose you are not surprised for me to suggest we count some numbers....counting with me in your mind.....because counting takes you deeper.... deeper down....like stepping down a staircase..... this counting thing gives your conscious mind something to do....that conscious mind that is used to being so busy chasing after this thought and that.......but by giving your conscious mind something to do....something steady.... pursuing just the one pattern of thought.....not a myriad of thoughts it allows that busy mind to quieten down and eventually become still.....giving you some peace from the stormy sea of your thought sodden mind....so let's get on with it you might be saying..... let us start this counting thing so that your thoughts stop swirling and wondering about what will happen next.... so let us count in a very specific way, ... would like you to see a book in front of you....never mind about the cover it is what is inside that counts.....

Opening the book and perhaps to your surprise the pages are blank, one blank page after another....if you ever saw words upon those pages they haven't fallen off now leaving the pages blank.... blank and crisp like new....so how about imagining now and we start counting backwards from 200....seeing the number 200 appear on the page......is it in the middle or the corner perhaps? It is your book..... just see the number there and then the counting begins....turning the page and it says 199.....then another page and it is 198 as you continue turning the pages and seeing the numbers there....the numbers going backwards.... backwards counting down......197 then over the page 196.... seeing the numbers 195....the curve of the numbers......194, then it is 193.... as you continue to relax 192.... deeper and deeper 191.. and then the page says 190 and you can keep turning the pages and seeing the numbers there.....counting down....taking yourself down to that quiet place when the conscious mind can slow right down....

If you fumble with the pages you can start again....wherever in the book you want, but keep the pages turning and the numbers going back down.... the rhythm of the pages turning and the numbers going down taking you right down now to a quiet place.....a still place where there is no more need of the numbers and you can drift with my words and follow my words on the pathway of change we have set out upon today....as you drift and your dream that conscious mind was once like a hamster on a wheel turning and turning and chasing and chasing and now it has climbed off the wheel and curled up in the corner amongst the sawdust and cotton wool....it can rest and allow my words to drift through to that subconscious mind that great powerhouse of a subconscious mind to create change for you today...

Candelabra

I would like you to imagine you are in an elaborate Dining room with two candelabras in the middle of a dining table... the table may be set for a meal... there are five candles in each candelabra..... I wonder what colour the candles are...... and the candelabras........ are they made of wood...... of silver or even of gold... seeing them clearly in the candle light... perhaps shimmering in the candle light.... seeing the flickering of the candles as a slight draft moves through the room.............in a moment I would like you to go over to the dining table and you are going to blow out the candles one at a time.....so going over to the table now and blowing out the 10th candle, perhaps scenting the smell of the wax as the candle gutters out and you feel a sweeping sense of relaxation move through you as the candle goes out......blowing out the 9th candle now......and relaxing deeper and deeper with each candle that you blow out...blow out the 8th candle now.......as the room shimmers in the candle light....you relax deeper down...... down deeper ...as you blow out the 7th candle...... so restful the light in the room now and you drift deeper.....blowing out the 6th candle now...such a relief, one candelabra has been done now and you relax twice as much again....over to the other candelabra now and blow out the 5th candle....so comfortable and relaxed now.... with each candle that goes out feeling yourself drift deeper into trance now....only four candles left now.....so blowing out that fourth candle.....deeper and deeper....and the third candle now.... and the room is darker now....which is so relaxing...so calming..... the gentle flickering... two candles left...blowing out the second candle now...feeling your breathing so relaxed now and blowing out the first and last candle and as the room goes into a soft and gentle velvety darkness you feel yourself goes deeply into trance now...that's right.

Sports

You are watching a game of tennis....out in the open.... a grass court..... not a game where you are particularly concerned about the outcome..... just watching....not a great game.....just passing the time watching the ball moves from side to side as you watch from the edge of the court...... back and forth....... back and forth... relaxing deeper and deeper......... hearing the ball hit the racket...... the sound of the ball whizzing through the air...the rhythm of the ball taking you deeper and deeper..back and forth.......back and forth.......15 – love....... deeper and deeper....... watching the ball ......seeing it bounce.......15 all...... deeper down into relaxation........a long volley back and forth....... back and forth... and the score changes again....15 – 30........ relaxing with the rhythm of the game.............. relaxing down.......back and forth...... following the ball.....back and forth.......30 all... the warmth of the sun on your face....the repetition of that sound of the ball bouncing on....the.... grass...............ball on racket....... back and forth ....40-30........service.....deeper down......game over.....so deep now.....that's right.....

Depression

Depression – Car Battery

Depression is a word we hear a lot about and it means different things for different people.....but for most of us it feels stuck..... stuck in a place we cannot see out of, the bottom of a hole........at the bottom of a hole and we cannot even be bothered to look and see if a ladder is there.......because even if there is one it will probably be too short.....or that is how it feels.....no way out..... do not pass go, do not collect two hundred pounds......stuck and just no energy, sapped and drained with all the juice squeezed out.....nothing left to give.....sometimes it is because something has happened and sometimes it descends from nowhere....I always remember the line from Keats which compared the sudden onset of melancholy...misery....like that of a storm erupting above you a sudden burst of rain ......says it to me.......suddenly drenched through to the skin when you were out there trying to have a good time.........

But what is it about the choices we have....sometimes there are choices....ways to dig our way out of that hole....

I see it like a flat battery.....not a spark of life in it.....do you feel like that sometimes? 0 power....nothing left....but plug in that battery and you can re-charge it....just a flicker at first of course, a flicker of life that builds and surges and then is back to full strength.....or what about a different kind of battery......what about when the battery of your car goes flat......you turn the key in the engine and it just will not start....instead of a long old charge you can get some jump leads.....you can get those jump leads and connect them to another battery one with some power still in it and you can use those leads to spark your own engine alive........ I wonder what it feels like to be that engine suddenly sparking with power........ with energy.......all you have to do is keep that engine running for a while.......take it for a spin and it is back on the road again.......you are back on the road again........ we can do that now..........can you feel it.....the energy returning yet......just imagine it at first...imagine that first spark.......... I wonder when you will notice........feel that first spark of interest.......can you feel it now....the power resurgent or will it take longer, a sudden re-start or a slow charge....... but you have started that process by being here today, by plugging into a new way of doing things, for looking for the way out, the ladder was there all along you just could not see it in the dark.......you see it now and you are on your way out......I wonder when you will feel that glimmer or change or will it be a burst of change..... I do not know when but you have started the process today, you are on your way.

Depression – Modelling

So many things as we go through life....patterns or behaviours you hear those words, nature or nurture, I cannot help it we say.....my Dad was just like it or my Mum did that.......... but how much is really in the genes and how much is just us copying them I wonder....I wonder that.......you see when we are tiny children we learn what we need to know about the world from our parents..........we do not have this thing called a critical faculty......we do not question their truth.......their truth of the world around us they present to us.....that is just how it is.......we see their reflection of the world and believe it to be true.......it is how we learn what to do.......we copy how they talk.......perhaps how they walk.....what to do when people are around........we spend those early years absorbing our parents like a sponge........ so, for example when in one house a parent sees a spider and they scream that child learns it is something to be afraid of and in the house next door the parent picks up the spider in a glass with a piece of card to secure it and they learn not to be afraid............. we get this because it is so obvious........it is tangible........we can see the results of this learning we do.......one step further and

anxious parent is likely to create an anxious child...............
absorbing the fears........learning from the parent so much
fear.......so what about depression....... could it not be that you
learned it too........learned not to delight in things, not to feel the
joyful moments or to just snuff them out...........I am just
wondering if you can see the pattern..........because if we have
learned something we can unlearn it and find a new way........... a
new way of doing things, we unlearn all sorts of things in
life...........beliefs of childhood as we become adults, we get taught
about Father Christmas or Santa Claus but I would be surprised if
you had not unlearned that one........so what about unlearning
depression what about finding a new model for your life...........is
there someone you know you would like to be like?...........
someone who seems happier in their life even though it is not
always perfect..........what is different about them?.....how do
they do it?........what is their body language?.......what is their
facial expression?.......what kind of words do they use?........I
would like you to think about that for a while........

Would you rather be like them than your parents?.....who would
you like to be?.......you modelled your current model years ago,
how about trading it in.......finding a new model....... if you think
about it.......it can be true....... I am going to give you some time
to think about what someone you know could do differently.....
how could you stand differently?....... choose different words,
create your new reality...........that's right, choosing a new way, a
new model.....become it, model it, become it and day by day
notice the changes occurring as people react differently to you......
..I wonder when you will realise you are not acting any more, not
modelling any more but this is actually you, a new and more
contented you.

Depression – Nature

Depression can be caused by a life situation.....if it is a life
situation.....then where possible it is about changing that life
situation.......or at least changing your response to it........you

41

can actively choose to stay in a situation or you can actually choose to leave it....then there is depression that you have learned, learned from a parent or from someone close to you......... learned that the glass is perpetually half empty and have overlooked that it can be refilled.......but that is all understandable..........adaptable and changeable.

But what about that other form of depression.......what if it is really physical.......brain chemistry. An inherited disorder perhaps, just not enough serotonin, not enough of those feel good chemicals in the brain..........what then, taking tablets forever to raise them up........put those missing chemicals back in perhaps and there is nothing wrong with that..........only there is a different way to raise those chemicals........ a way that means one day maybe you can stop taking the tablets as you take control for yourself........ you see our mind and our body are connected, there are Yogis in India who can turn anti bodies on and off in their blood stream, they can slow their heart rates down so they could live in an environment with barely any oxygen for a while,.....how else do people walk across burning coals or lie on a bed of nails if they are not in some way controlling that mind and body response, I guess I am telling you things you may have heard........ but these are Yogis in India and other far flung shores who spend years perfecting their body control.......but you do it in small ways and in bigger ways every day....... a therapist long ago called Milton Erickson when talking about pain, pointed out that we lose the awareness of the sensations in our feet.......... the shoes upon our feet until someone mentions it and suddenly we are aware again.......there was no anaesthetic there.....we just altered our focus, but that is just a shift of a attention, what about something a bit more tangible........some people find their mouth water just by thinking of lemon juice trickle over their tongue........or indeed the prospect of a wonderful meal, people can get aroused, have physical symptoms of arousal just by thinking an erotic thought, there is a suggestibility test we sometimes do that gets you to imagine you are holding a heavy book in one hand and have balloons tied to the other whilst your eyes are closed and do you

know most people find their arms rising or falling as a result.......
rising with the balloons and falling with the books.....most
people.........ordinary people like you and I, not yogis in
India........just average people having a simple thought affect their
body.....

So if all this is true.........you may also know when you think a
positive thought it releases all the good endorphins into your
blood stream.......if you worry it releases stress hormones and if
you think sad thoughts it releases the appropriate hormones and
our minds you know cannot tell the difference between the
thought and the reality........what we think, so we become, so
here is the new thought.....you can think up your serotonin levels,
you can create them yourself,.....what can you think about that
might just begin to trigger that production line in your brain........
pumping out that serotonin for you, even if you inherited that
deficit.......you can work on it, make it stronger like working out
a muscle and building it up.

I wonder what would make you happier, what thought can take
you there, let us think on that for a while.........or maybe just
imagine that serotonin level in your brain getting going again......
like the workers have been on strike but they are back in action
again and those neurones in the brain start sparking into life and
carry different messages around, can you look for, search for one
thought that might spark that production line off again, one
moment, past, or future, it does not matter, it will all do...........
just one moment of feeling better, think that thought.........not
dwelling on the bad stuff, leave that alone, it is like picking at a
scab.......let it heal and move those thoughts on, take control now
you can do it, I know it because I have seen just what people can
do to change their mind........just ordinary people like me and
you, seeing the way out......thinking their way out, just one small
thought can make that change and I wonder when you will feel
those levels rise, I wonder when, I wonder....

Food issues

Anorexia – The Garden

I would like you to imagine.... see in your mind's eye a walled garden with a wooden gate.... the bricks in the wall are reddish in colour.... the gate large and the wood engraved with patterns..... go through the wooden gate and see the garden spreading out in front of you...... looking to the right hand side of this garden, see the trees...... shrubs, beautiful flowers...... see the colours of the flowers..... you may even be aware of the scent of the flowers on the gentle breeze..... it is a warm summer's day..... feel the sun warming your skin, so soothing and relaxing and that gentle breeze ruffles your hair...... the grass so green beneath your feet and soft..... soft and springy beneath your feet.

The gardener of this garden had decided in the spring to do an experiment. The plants on the right hand side of this garden..... when they were planted as tiny seeds...... he placed them in the sunlight...... he put plant food in the earth...... he watered them devotedly every day..... tending them lovingly....... showing them care...... and they rewarded him by growing up from the soil...... unfurling their leaves and their petals...... so beautiful, they grew to be so beautiful under his tender care...... everyone entering the garden commented on the flowers...... how beautiful they looked.

The other half of the experiment you will see on the left hand side of this garden.......he planted some seeds in the shade...... plants take their energy...... their food from the sun....... so he deprived them of their natural source of energy........ and he did not put the plant food in the soil that he had given the other plants ....he often forgot to water these seeds............. he wondered what would happen if he did not look after those seeds.......... not take care of them..................not nourish them and water them............. While they struggled to grow..........they became ugly weedy shrunken plants............ not beautiful and blooming............... when people came into the garden they did not admire them..............they passed them by........... their colours were faded........... they did not have the energy to give the lovely perfume smells to the garden that the other plants could do.......after a couple of months like this the gardener felt sorry for those plants................ he moved them out of the shade into the sun.................

Replanting them and gave them some food................... he then watered them every time he watered the others and in time they began to bloom............. they responded to his care and the nourishment they could get from the sun and they became as beautiful as the other flowers............ that's right........... blooming and lovely.......... contributing a lovely smell to the garden.... contributing to the overall beauty of the garden. So it is time to take care of you now...to nourish you now....so that you can bloom, can blossom....not wither with starvation....but grow and be strong...strong and nourished like the beautiful plants...I know your subconscious understands, gets the link and takes it all in.

Weight Control – Casting Off

As you continue to relax as you listen to my voice....I would like you to imagine you are standing on a sandy beach....see the golden colour of the sand....feel the sand soft beneath your feet......see the blue of the sea....the blue of the sky....the hard line of the horizon where the sky and sea meet....you may hear the sound of the sea....rolling in....and out....in ....and out....smell the salty sea air....see seaweed lying on the sand...browns... reds....feel the sun warming your skin....on this beautiful summer's day...we all like that feeling...that soothing feeling of the sun warming our skin....that's right.....relaxing in the sun....

Now there is a boat close to the shore....you may not have seen it at first, but see it now......it is tied by a rope to a piece of wood in the sand...tethering the boat in case the water rises...so now go over to that boat....perhaps you feel a gentle breeze ruffling your hair as you make your way towards the boat....I want you to load into that boat all the foods that you do not want to eat any more.....fatty foods.....sweet foods....fattening drinks like cans of coke.... cans of beer....letting them go.....piling them into the boat....you do not want these foods in your life now...piling it up...so that when you leave here today...you have left them behind you...cast them off....cast those unhealthy foods away.... so that they drift far away from you and soon far out of your life....so finish loading the boat....piling the boat up.....then

Go over to the rope and untie it...throw the rope into the boat.... and if it needs it push the boat off the sand and into the sea....give it a good shove into the sea....put all your strength behind it... forcing it away from you.....you do not need these foods any more.....feel the tide catch the boat...pulling it out to sea....the current takes hold of the boat...pulling it further and further away....it lies heavy in the water........low in the water as it goes through the water..........drifting out to sea........watching it go....that breeze picks up....pulling the boat away from you..... taking all those unwanted foods away...so you can leave them now....you can find new ways of doing things...the boat becomes smaller and smaller as it nears the horizon....until it is a small dot on the horizon....and suddenly it is gone....you feel freer and lighter....so much easier....liberated from those old ways... looking towards the future now....leaving here today having let go...cast away all the old habits and behaviours around food, as you do not need them anymore....Then you notice in the distance another boat coming into view from a different direction........ perhaps it may surprise you this new boat as it seems to be heading straight towards you, as if it knew you were there and were coming to visit you.........someone is calling from the boat, they are calling to you.....the boat pulls up and it is full of fresh and healthy foods....fruits and vegetables...salads and pulses...fresh fish...all the healthy foods that you want to eat now...delivered to you now....especially for you now.....that's right.....

Alternative uses for this script

This script can be adapted to address other addictions.

Alcohol: A client with alcohol issues could put all the alcohol they would have drunk in the coming month in the boat and cast it away, they could alternatively put all the empty bottles or cans from the previous month or months in the boat, to get a sense of the scale of their drinking and cast that away, to place it in the past.

Cigarettes: A smoker can place a month's worth of cigarettes in the boat and cast that away.

Relationships: Someone with addiction to a past relationship or even unrequited love, could place the person in the boat and let them sail away, a new boat could come into view, showing a new person come into their life, it is best to leave the boat far enough away to not see the identity of the person in the boat, but just give a sense that a new relationship is on the horizon and heading their way.

Weight Control – Mindful

Now when you start to prepare food and to eat food you are going to slow down and do this eating properly......eating with choice and awareness.....notice the sensation of touch in your fingertips......all those tiny nerve endings giving you your sense of touch....... feel and think about the feeling, when you are eating food or preparing food, be aware of this sensation of touch, it can be the touch of your hands or the sensation of touch on your lips and tongue.....aware of that feeling....is it greasy?....not wanting greasy sensations on your hands or lips....aware of not liking that greasy feeling....or the sensation....the cloying sensation of sugary foods....no longer just bolting food down...but aware of the feeling the sensations of the food....wanting foods that feel fresh and crisp....not oily...not sugary....aware of not liking that oily...

greasy sensation on your lips...on your hands...something you had overlooked before...because you ate without thinking... without awareness...but you are aware now...and you will not overlook it now...

When you are cooking your food now... Listen carefully.... focus....focus on the sound.....the sound of your food....as you cook...is it sizzling?....that frying sizzling sound...so invasive ...so disturbing...fat flying off the pan...hearing the sizzle...no longer wanting that sizzling sound...because that sizzling sound means food is unhealthy...an unhealthy sound....aware of the sizzle of fat...fat that will end up on your body...melding itself to your body...not a sound you want to hear any more...what about that crisp sound of chopping vegetables and preparing vegetables, a healthy sound...liking that sound...

Now what can you see?...when you look at your food...see the vibrant healthy colours ...natural colours of good food....not wanting to see food that is laden with fat and sugar...because you can see yourself just getting bigger and bigger...having that awareness .....aware of what you see...how the food looks...real food...not processed food...as you begin to feel smell and see food...gaining pleasure from preparing the food....

Knowing how good it will be for you...trying different foods....

And now taste...so important taste...slowing down your eating so you really taste your food...rolling it around your mouth as you chew. Getting the textures and flavours....not wanting fatty... sugary ...cloying foods....that taste...distasteful to you now... because you are thinking about what you eat...not just shovelling food in without a care...just piling food in without noticing it... noticing how good healthy food tastes...fresh...clean flavours.... slowing down the process so you eat mindfully....knowing what you are eating...taking care of what you eat...taking care of you now....and as you eat with focus...with deliberation...you will eat healthy food....as why would you deliberately...carefully eat fatty foods...foods that will make you fat...you would not choose to be fat and unhealthy...because you are choosing what you eat now... eating with deliberation...you are what you eat...you have heard that before but now you know what it means as you eat with focus and choice...becoming a mindful eater

Alternative uses for this script.

Alcohol dependency: Utilising the idea of being mindful about what we put in our body can be applied to alcohol, if the client becomes aware of what they are doing and not mindlessly consume alcohol anymore, they can begin to make active choices, choosing cleansing refreshing water for example and linking this in to health benefits, rather than the alcohol which is damaging the body, tuning in to the damage to the liver, creating a mindful awareness of the impact upon the body and emphasising the choice the body would make, leading to a mind/body awareness informing the client's choice over what he/she drinks.

Habits

Trichotillomania (Hair-pulling) – The Lawn

I would like you to imagine a lawn in a garden, a green lawn, see the shade of green, the strands of the grass so neatly cut......the perfect rolling lawn.....the scent perhaps of freshly cut grass, I wonder if you can notice that, the lawn looks as good as it is possible to look, if you neglect it, if you leave it for months on end it would look over grown, a mess, unkempt and unloved, I wonder if you have seen a lawn just like that, it almost feels it can get too long to cut....... so it is important to let the lawn get to just the right length to for that perfect cut..........that perfect trim......now if you start to cut too soon, if the grass is not at the same even length........it can end up looking patchy and uneven....... I wonder if you have noticed that, a gardener always knows when the lawn has reached just the right length to cut it........no need to yank the grass out by the roots creating unsightly bald patches....... with buts of red earth showing through......just leave it be, let it grow to just the right length and then you can get that lovely even finish...... if you are in any doubt how long to leave it you can always get a professional opinion, ask an expert and they will help you to have the perfect lawn, I think you have found your expert......... you know who to ask, they have told you what to do, no need to pull at the roots yourself......leave it to the expert and your deep unconscious mind that holds all those habits and behaviours can understand this message........take the information it needs from it to ensure that from now on you leave that hair alone....... leave it to the expert to deal with it, it is what they are there for......I know you know now what you need to do, you do not need me to remind you that you will leave those hairs alone and if at any moment you find your hand wandering there you can make the right choice, you can choose what to do and I know that you will choose now, to leave that hair alone.

You have the awareness now in that powerful unconscious mind and it knows now what you want it to do and what not to do, that's right. As you allow yourself to relax back into the image of that beautiful green lawn..... lush....even........like a stretching sheet of velvet..... green velvet..........that is right and you know what is right for you now........so perhaps now you have taken the time to create this beautiful green lawn, you can lie down upon it and feel the softness beneath you.......and look up at the sky and the clouds scudding by and enjoy this moment of relaxation and take this new learning back with you today when you awaken, that's right.

Trichotillomania – The Shrubbery

The hair is soft and smooth like the petal of a flower.....feel that texture.... I want you to really be aware when you touch your hair of the smoothness of it, the silky texture of it.......as you are relaxing here now.....remember the texture and the feel of it.....I wonder why you would want to pull it.... to hurt your sensitive skin...... that smooth and sensitive skin.....now I would like you to come on a journey with me......just following me into the garden......a lovely garden with very neat flower beds, they look beautiful, those flowers..... I wonder what colours they are? What kinds of flowers you can see?....... The lawn is neatly clipped and a shimmering green..... the ground, the soil that holds the plants..... so neatly hoed and raked over....so neat, seeing the colour of the soil......the stems of the flowers...long and sleek perhaps or shorter more abundant bloom..........just take some time to admire the garden......perhaps feeling the softness of the grass beneath your feet......admiring your creation.....you may not have realised you were capable of such a wonderful creation... admiring it...... a well manicured garden, well maintained and cared for, work you can be proud of........I will be quiet for a few moments just to let you enjoy it, enjoying the flowers, the long stems, the colours all around.

It is time to leave the garden for now as the day is passing and the light is fading, the beautiful sun slipping away and it is time to rest, relax.......as you drift deeper and deeper with each breath you take......the sun sets over the garden and a day is done, a new day lies ahead of you, a new day to return and relax in your garden....yes......another day comes and you want to return to your garden, I want you to imagine a new fresh morning and going back into the garden but whilst you have been away..... someone has been in your garden and pulled some of your beautiful plants....pulled them out by the roots.....just wrenched them out, they lie strewn around the ground, broken, your beautiful garden.....with all that work you put in destroyed, damaged, not so beautiful anymore, it can be replanted, but it hurts to see it destroyed, damaged and hurt.........

But it can grow again, you replant the garden....taking care of the soil....watering and nourishing the garden, caring for it to bring it back to its former glory..... this time I know you will watch over the garden, make sure it is safe and secure.....that no one can break in and damage your tender plants and wreck what is yours, on guard from now on, on guard for that attack upon the garden.....

On guard for that attack upon your hair....no one and nothing will damage it now, accept a professional gardener perhaps just trimming it back....I know that you will take care of it now, tend it and take care of it, for you will be aware, aware if your hand goes to you hair, you can touch it and brush it......tend it and take care of it but nothing and no one will make you vandalise it...... because tearing it out would be vandalism, no other word for it.... destroying, damaging, now you want to take care of it, enjoying washing it, conditioning it.....keeping it in prime condition and no one will hurt it, you will not hurt it, you take pride in it, tending and caring for it, you are in control now.......in control of your hands and you can touch your hair, caring for it, ...feel its soft texture.........but nothing now will make you pull at it, damage it, you just care of it as you would care of that garden, that's right, that is in the past now, damaging and hurting your hair is in the past, enjoying the touch of it, aware of the feel of it and keeping it safe, that's right.....

Heart Condition

Tachycardia – The Steam Train

A couple of weeks ago..... I meant to tell you.....I was walking through the countryside.......... I saw huge plumes of smoke rising high in the air.... far in the distance.......such a roaring sound in the distance too......I walked towards the smoke to see what could be causing all that noisy steam....and there was an old steam train....just like you see at the pictures....going clickety click.....clickety click along the tracks.....speeding through the countryside....clickety click..... powering that train along.... clickety click.........I could see the beautiful Pulman carriages....in brown and cream.....clickety click..........as the train plunged on through the countryside powered by the steam....clickety click...... steaming along the tracks....clickety click.....and then the screeching sound as more steam was released.....then clickety click....powering along the tracks...clickety click......and if the train is a little too fast approaching that bend.....clickety cick.........releasing even more steam and slowing her down..... slowing her right down....clickeeeerty click ....if it is going too fast.....too much pressure.....must let of that steam.....and relax the tension ....clickeeeeerty click....taking control and slowing her down......clickeeeeerty click....

Always able to control that pressure....following the rhythm and taking control....slowing her right down ......that's right....you can take control.....following the natural rhythm and releasing the pressure....your subconscious knows what to do now.....allow the subconscious mind learn all it needs to.....from the stories you hear....acquiring new learnings in your subconscious mind.....as you slow it down to a steady gentle rhythm.....no more skipping beats .....no more fast beats but a steady gentle rhythm....and your subconscious mind knows all it needs to do now....releasing that pressure and feeling better.....following the natural rhythm.....pacing along....your own internal pacemaker....setting that rhythm now....trusting your subconscious mind to take care of you now....tick tock following the clock.....safe and secure now.....tick tock follow the clock....and remembering all these new learnings now.....

Heart condition – The Farmer

It reminds me of a story of a farmer I once knew....he had a small farm where he kept horses...horses that needed pasture to graze.... but he lived in a very dry area....he had to keep his fields well irrigated....he invested in an expensive pump to look after the land....he did this as a young man .....when he first bought the farm.....it cost him so much that pump....it was state of the art.... top of the range....he just left it to get on with its job....sending the water around the fields....keeping the land lush....he did not even bother to check if it was working....he paid so much for it... he did not think it needed any attention.....but all things need care and attention.....need to be looked after....no matter how good they are at the start....when they are shiny and new.....things that work hard day after day.....they need care and attention....not to be taken for granted.....as the farmer did that pump....one day he noticed the grass was no longer lush and green....going brown around the edges.....so he went to check the pump....it had stopped as he had not been checking on it, getting it serviced each year as the warranty said he should....he just took it for granted.... he got someone in to fix the pump....he had relied on the steady pumping of that pump to send the water around the fields for years and it had always done its job....keeping the fields lush and rich for the horses to graze.

When the pump was repaired the farmer vowed he would never take that pump for granted again....he had it serviced every year and looked after it with care....and that pump never let him down again....he worried for a while after that one time....but soon he realised he could trust the pump again....as he now took good care of it....every other day of that pump's working life it had done its job well...it had worked perfectly.....it stopped to remind the farmer to take care of it....and that care, kept that pump going year upon year....it was just a small warning to take care of it.... like the warning light in your car comes on to let you know there is a problem....once the problem is fixed you can trust it again.... to take care of you....take you wherever it is that you want to go...and your subconscious mind can learn all of this and more... as you relax and allow the subconscious mind to learn all it needs to from this to keep you well and strong....taking care and aware.....learning to trust the pump again....

IBS

When treating IBS it is important to focus on relaxation, so any script that will induce relaxing will be helpful, but below are some metaphorical ideas that will help IBS sufferers.

IBS – Pooh Sticks

Did you ever read the Winnie the Pooh books when you were a child......or perhaps read them as an adult..........many people have seen the Disney film. In one of the books Christopher Robin accidentally drops a pine cone over a bridge and he watches as it appears on the other side of the bridge..........Christopher Robin then devises the game of Pooh Sticks which he plays with Tigger and EEyore.......fierce competition between the characters develops as each character throws his stick in the water, wants his stick to be the first to appear from under the bridge..........rushing from one side to the other to see......who will be first.........who will win this time...... I wonder if you ever played pooh sticks when you were a child ....or even as an adult when connecting with the child within.........sometimes, just sometimes the stick never appears again from under the bridge.......... it has got snagged on something in the water............perhaps a bush leaning out from the shore, so you need to go down to the water and dislodge the trapped stick from it to return to its journey down the river..........ok, you have not won the game but releasing the stick is part of completing the game....... even if you did not go to release it the swell of the current, the pressure of the tidal flow will release that stick and it will flow easily again on it's journey down the river........a slow and gentle flow or a fast race to the next bend in the river....... always carrying on its journey in the end.......will the journey lead out to the open sea I wonder.........in the end I guess it will.

I sometimes think it is a bit like untying a knot........sometimes we rush at it, pull and tug and strain at it and the knot just seems to get tighter.........it pulls tighter and tighter and we struggle with it.......yet if we patiently....... slowly and carefully approached that knot.........our fingers do not stumble....... it unties with ease...... but every knot can be untied in the end........it reminds me of a saying I have heard many times.........the harder you try to do something, the more difficult it becomes, rather like trying to remember someones name........in the middle of a conversation you look for that name and a chasm opens up in front of you, a yawning chasm.......empty........empty of the word you want..... no matter how hard you hunt it just will not come......yet, when you stop trying......stop hunting for that name........up it pops, like a cork popping up to the surface through water.....up the name surges........just because you have stopped trying so hard...... stopped thinking about it, letting the natural flow of thoughts bring you the name........like the natural flow of the river releases the stick, it flows down to the sea.

I guess the answer is to just relax and go with the flow........ the more attention you give it the harder it becomes......relaxing all your muscles and allowing the natural flow to occur.......the ebb and surge of the tide......the tides within you...... letting them take care of you, the harder you try, the more difficult it becomes....... so leave the trying behind you and relax......every knot can be untied, the natural flow restored and your subconscious mind understands the meanings of my words and the stories that I tell.............seeing the message within........the hidden nugget that you can take away to look at later........ in your subconscious mind.......understanding occurs and the muscles relax.......the discomfort ebbs away........the natural flow returning. Allowing the muscles to relax, perhaps seeing them loosening up and letting go......when I think about my muscles.......my muscles relaxing... ....I imagine smoothing them out......like rolling out pastry..... seeing the lumps and bumps go away smoothed away, all tensions in those muscles gone, so they can work easily, that gentle flow returning.......tensions eased, pain gone, as you let go and take your attention elsewhere, just as you do when searching for the word......withdraw your attention from the search, from the effort of it and it effortlessly comes along........ the result that you want...........and you have learned so much more about relaxing........relaxing your mind and your body.......letting the thoughts drift on by........not engaging with them.......those worrying thoughts........letting them pass right by.......like the train you do not board as it chases through the station just leaving that roar behind......the whistle of air gushing past......letting it go......letting the thoughts go by and relax.......you know just what to do now........you have learned new ways......no more worry and fret.......letting it go now.....releasing, letting go and the gentle flow returns.

IBS Pain – The Pastry

If you feel that pain.......that discomfort........I would like you to go on a particular journey with me.......visualise a kitchen.......an old fashioned kitchen....... with pots and pans hanging on the wall over an old cooking range......they might be copper pans, or indeed any kind of pans........there is an old kettle on top of the range.......ready for boiling a cup of tea when you have finished here........you may have seen such a kitchen in a film or if you have visited a country house........it would look like that........but of course any kitchen will do.......it really does not matter what the kitchen looks like....... all it needs is a table......the kitchen does need a table, my table is an old pine one......years of preparation for cooking have gone on here....... but any table will do....put in the middle of the table a large piece of dough.....the kind of dough for making pastry, the flour and the water and the butter are already blended together into a large sticky piece of dough and the dough sits there in the middle of the table........... there is flour sprinkled across the top of the table to stop the dough from sticking to it........now look at the lump of dough and put the pain inside it.......that's right....... just imagine the pain and transmit the pain into that lump of dough.....sitting there on top of the table.......imagine it is there......sense it is there....... now pick up the rolling pin........you may not have noticed it there........is the rolling pin wooden?

I used to have a glass one, anyway......see it now and pick it up and start to roll out the dough......starting by placing the pressure on the middle of the dough and gradually rolling it into a flat piece of pastry......it is lumpy and bumpy at first, rolling backwards and forwards.......backwards and forwards........backwards and forwards with the rolling pin.......smoothing out the bumps spreading the pastry and pushing out the pain.......spreading the dough across the table........squeezing out the pain, flattening it out.....smoothing it out......it reaches the edges and then slips away, rolling out that pastry until it is paper thin......no more lumps and bumps you have soothed them away.......push them out........relieved to have taken control of it.......pushed it out, smoothed it out......... the pasty is ready now......ready for whatever you want to bake........the pain turned to discomfort as you rolled it out........flattened it out and then disappeared......you squeezed it out at the edges those lumps and bumps gone.......you can do this whenever you want to, when the pain starts just put it into the lump of pastry and take control of it smooth it out........ feeling the rolling pin under your hands......perhaps remembering what the pastry might smell like, hearing the sound of the pin rolling, soothing......letting it go now, letting it go....I wonder when you will notice that it has gone, driven out, forced out..... squeezed out........ like squeezing the juice out of an orange....... you can squeeze it out, push it out and be rid of the pain...anytime you want to now...you can do this for you and let it go.

Alternative uses for this script

Muscle pain: The concept of smoothing out the lumps and bumps in pastry can also be applied to any muscle problems and cramping.

IBS – Physical

As you relax there I want you to think about the complex machine that is your body..........that takes in nutrition and processes it and passes out the waste........it is an incredible piece of engineering and every single cell needs to play it's part in the process..........we need to think about the fuel we take on board.........the right nutrients for us and I am sure you do not need me to tell you what to eat or when to eat........when to eat a large meal........ not late at night of course.......you know all about that.......you know about eating the right foods and the foods that are not helpful to you.........I wonder if you can imagine your body working through the processing of that carefully chosen food and drink........imagine how each part needs to fulfil its purpose........perhaps for a while there has been a fault in the system......but we are correcting that now....... the wrong messages had got through, the messages that made it all too fast or far too slow........because your brain needs to tell your digestive system what to do..........give it the right instructions, you can make sure the right messages get through........the gentle rhythm of your inner body......the muscles creating the gentle steady rhythm, that moves the food through your system........... carrying it along through the small intestine into the large........ absorbing just the right amount of fluid.......moving steadily, along a steady pulse of digestion like the steady pulse of your heart.......the in and out of the breath......... the expansion and contraction of the muscles that take the food along......not too fast......not too slow.....that's right.......you can tell your body what to do.......to follow that steady rhythmic pace.......taking the food on it's journey, taking the nutrients that it needs until all that is left is the waste products......which you can release and let go of.......all at a steady pace......a gentle pace.....not too fast, not too slow.......following the natural flow of your body.

You can take control, as you stay so relaxed now......when we stay relaxed, the body understands what to do.......... if we move into fight or flight response, the blood flow gets diverted from that digestive system.......leaving it unsupported.......unable to process the food easily....... unable to carry it along..........it either gets rid of it quickly.......passing it on too fast so you do not get the nutrients you need, or it stops........comes to a halt......a freeze in the process......halting all, until the storm is passed.......the crisis is passed......so keeping relaxed and calm.......choosing calming and relaxing thoughts actually helps your body.......helps your body to do what it needs to do......to get the nourishment it needs and let the rest pass through, so what are you going to do now, will you help your body now......seeing it working smoothly and easily......all flowing through.....like the steady flow of a river...... or maybe the canals of old.......taking their goods from one place to another.....a steady flow like that canal........just waiting at the lock, for the right moment and then on it goes........as you wait at the lock and then it is the time to go...... letting go, no pain or discomfort now, because you have controlled the flow.

Inductions

We can use metaphors within our inductions, it can help reduce the resistance of the client, it is rather like settling down to a bedtime story, though the first example a confusing one to encourage a quick switch off, for the conscious mind.

Confusion Induction

You can close your eyes now or later if you wish...........it is up to you, though to follow what I say it may be easier to let them drift shut............ remembering how comfortable it is to have your eyes closed as you listen to my voice and the things that I say to you.............And if I asked you to think about your body.......... to focus on your body............. you may think about your nose........... a foot......an ear or a finger........ a jaw or an eye..............who knows.......Only your subconscious knows where to go......... to the left or the right......... choices........ choices.....

And if seven men choose to push four carts the five miles home it takes a couple of hours....But will six men with three carts do it in two minutes ten...Or if one sprains their ankle and five are left for the pushing.....but they decide to leave one cart behind to collect it later........ will they be home by six,........ or will it be seven and how about eleven carts........... so many carts and not enough men for the pushing of the carts all the miles home..............You may be aware or unaware now of the meaning of my words and the distance of the carts as they travel that long road home as you drift in and out of awareness.......Two and two make four and four by four is the best way to travel on that bumpy track home............. not the pushing of carts laden with oranges as some fall off and roll into a ditch...................

And sometimes when you talk............lost in the talk............yes means no and no means yes and when to know which is right and which is wrong...........right is the turning home or is it the third on the left...so many choices as you drift deeper down. No need to try to follow your conscious mind as it drifts on its journey.............. though stop at the red light and pass at the green and the amber lies someplace in between............... but you know where to go now as you drift and you dream as just three men are left to push those carts on the long road home..... but now you do not care............. not a care left........... as you drift along your own gentle road to a place of relaxing................ a place of dreaming and drifting all the way down............. deeper down now............. all the way down as you listen to my voice and follow your dreams as your conscious mind goes where it will...............dreaming and drifting.............drifting and dreaming, that's right.....Just listening to my words now with that subconscious mind and allowing the subconscious mind to take you to just the level of trance that you need to be to do all that you need to do for you right now.

Metaphor Induction

As you close your eyes and begin to relax, ... just begin to relax......thoughts may pass through your mind,.......drift through your mind..... like clouds scudding across the sky...... on a summer's day........... the blue of the sky............. and white fluffy clouds scudding across the sky on a breezy day............... allowing the thoughts to pass by...............drift by........... not engaging with them.............allowing them to pass on by as you begin to drift down............. drifting down deeper........... deeper into relaxation......... deeper down......... drifting........... drifting with the clouds as they scud across the sky....allowing those thoughts to pass by ...you do not need them now...clouds passing by....thoughts drifting by....

As your mind begins to let go....that conscious mind can let go.... and drift with your thoughts....your body can just begin to relax too....any tension you hold in your body....we often hold that tension in our upper body.....allowing that tension to drain away....allowing any tension in the body to drain away....like water draining away....draining down....and draining away.... seeing the water flow....and seeing it drain away....so relaxed now....as the muscles loosen and relax ....as the tension drains out of them drains away....relaxed in your mind and your body... all that tension draining away...draining down the plughole... taking it away taking any tension away.....

And now you have let your mind begin to relax .... the tension to drain down through your body....I would like you to imagine....see yourself on a beach....a sandy beach.....seeing the yellow of the sand....the golden yellow of the sand or perhaps just aware of the softness of the sand beneath your feet.....hearing the sound of the sea....as it rolls in.....and out.....as it rolls in....and out....you may be aware of the sound of seagulls....the sound of seagulls overhead....circling in the sky.....the tide rolling up the beach...the white surf unfurling.....up the beach and withdrawing again.....aware of the rhythm...that gentle rhythm of the tide as it surges in and withdraws....

The sun may be warm upon your skin...relaxing warmth...the warmth of the sun...soothing and relaxing you....no one here to expect anything of you ....no one to let you down.......nothing to do now.......just relaxing into the time...time for you on the beach....as you are aware of the sun....the sun is lowering in the sky....the amazing colours of a sunset...pinks....reds...oranges... that ball if fire...that fiery sun slowing sinking in the sky....making its way down....down towards the horizon....taking you deeper down into trance now.....the sun moving closer to that blue horizon....that hard blue line of the horizon...where the sky and sea meet ....the sun touching it now...and then slipping down....down behind the horizon now.....taking you down into trance now....as you watch the sun slipping down behind the horizon now.....slipping down into trance now....deep down into a relaxing trance now...so relaxed...peaceful and relaxed....as your conscious mind slips away now....drifts away somewhere else now....your subconscious mind taking care of you now.....it is going to do some work for you now....to help you....to do the work it needs to do for you today.....

Mindful Induction.

Feel the chair supporting you, aware of where your body touches the chair....... feeling supported...... safe...... sinking down..... into the chair....... releasing your muscles and letting go..... aware now of your breath....... where does your breath start?...... where do you notice it?...... the very beginning of your breath....... is the first movement in your diaphragm?........ or your chest?....... where do those muscles move and expand?...... expanding your chest...... sucking the air into your lungs...... filling them with air..... from the bottom..... filling them up to the top...... as you breathe in .... do the diaphragm and chest move together?........... where else do you feel movement?........... the rib cage expanding perhaps........... expanding and lifting a little........... allowing the air in........... where else do you notice movement?.............. your back, your shoulders?............. do they lift a little?................rising a little with each breath,........... can you feel the cool air on your top lip?.............. the cool air touching your top lip as your chest expands.............. pulling the air in........the air warming in your lungs........ as it releases the oxygen to be taken off around your body.............. collecting the carbon dioxide and breathing it out..............releasing it............ the warm air in your throat........... the warm air touching the top lip.......... before joining the atmosphere.......... slightly damp air released.........and the next breath again.............. but noticing perhaps that still moment.......... the stillness of your chest before you take your next breath...............that's right.......... how long is that pause?................ the pause between your out breath and the next breath in.............that nourishing breath in............deeper down now.......... then that diaphragm expands again.......... the chest rising............... the ribs lifting and separating.............. deeper down now.......the cool air rushing in.......... and the warm air flowing out and pausing.............aware of the movement................ any tension in our body now................

How are your hands? Any tension in your hands.......... where are they?............ and taking your attention back to your shoulders................ deeper down now.......allowing them to drop down a little with the out breath........... what about your feet?............... are your toes clenched together?..................... pressed together............ letting any tension there letting go.....................releasing your toes.............. releasing your fingers......... allowing the gentle flow of breaths in and out............. following the rhythm.............. that powerful rhythm................. the rhythm of life.................the flow of life in and out................. how long is the breath in?........... how long is the breath out?............... aware of your breath............... where it starts.................. following the flow of the breath................. the natural rhythm of the breath........... the flow of energy.............the flow of life............ aware of the life within you............ at one with your mind and your body............... deeper down now.......the synergy of your mind and your body.............. feeling completely aware.......in tune..... that's right.

Insomnia

When we are trying to sleep we are waiting for the conscious mind to switch off and the subconscious to take over, often the mind is so busy the subconscious does not get the signal, hence the development of the script which utilises the idea of the sleep trigger, which the subconscious is just waiting to receive. The other key factor with sleep is that law of the mind that the harder you try to do something the more difficult it becomes, the harder we try to sleep, the more awake we seem to become, the awareness of this truism can be utilised to tackle insomnia.

Insomnia – Chasing the Dog

I wonder if you have noticed that if you chase after a dog, it will run away from you and if you turn your back on it, it will return to your side....it is one of those natural rules....a horse will run if you move too quickly towards it.......or a sheep ....or a cow.......you have to tread gently ....softly.......or make it seem you are not interested at all.........life can be like that...... one of those golden rules.....the harder you try to do something the more difficult it becomes.....if you have forgotten a name....... or a word....if you chase it in your mind.......if you keep chasing around your mind........you rarely find it.....it is when you stop looking ......stop chasing.....that the word will pop into your mind.......like the faithful hound returning to your side.......sleep is a bit like that too......the harder you try to sleep......the more difficult it becomes........the more you think about sleep.......the more you chase sleep.......the further away it seems to get.....you become more and more awake.......so do not chase after sleep....... let it come to you......if you say to yourself it really does not matter....sleep can come.......or sleep can go.......it really does not matter to you......that is when your sleep will come and find you again......have you ever noticed........i wonder if you have noticed.......that time in the morning when you have hardly slept.......you look at your clock and there is just an hour or so......or half perhaps.......before that alarm will go......and just as you say...well that's it then......that is my lot for the night... ....I will stop trying to sleep now......that is when the sleep will come.......because you are not chasing it........you are not trying so hard, like leaving the search for the name and it pops into place.........because the harder you try the more difficult it becomes......if you chase that dog it will run away......or the naughty child........stop chasing and racing......just let it be and it will come to you.....sleep will come to you like your faithful hound........let it be........sleep will come......deep and refreshing sleep will come when you do not chase it......do not pressure it......just letting it be.......seeing that time in bed as time for you......just to rest and be......and along it will come.......deep and refreshing sleep......allowing it to come.......to keep you company through the night....that's right....

Insomnia – Falling Leaf

I would like you to imagine..... see yourself in a woodland scene...... walking through the woods.... perhaps there are twigs snapping underfoot.... the sound of birds singing in the trees.... the sound of a gentle breeze ruffling the trees and that smell of damp earth that pervades any woodland with a stream passing through..... perhaps hearing that stream in the distance.... find a tree that draws you to it........ a strong oak or a slender silver birch.....perhaps..... go over to that tree...... looking at it....... see the bark...... the textures.... the roots spreading across the ground and deep down into the soil...the colours of the woodland around you........ shades of browns and greens and perhaps mosses and ferns....fungi maybe around the base of the tree....

Sit down now with your back to the trunk of the tree.......look up into the canopy of leaves...... seeing the light dapple through the leaves as they shimmer in the breeze........ fluttering......... rustling........ and as you watch one leaf detaches itself and starts to flutter down towards the ground.......... watch that leaf as it

68

twists and turns in the light breeze........... as it moves down and down......... taking you down and down into restful sleep as you watch the leaf moving down and down.......... when you lie in your bed at night..........your subconscious mind will know that this is the signal......... when you are lying...comfortable in your bed at night....... that this is the sign to go to sleep..... the signal that the subconscious mind is waiting for to let it know that it is time to take over and allow the conscious mind to drift away somewhere else........somewhere where it can rest........ off to another place as it is not needed now.......... your subconscious mind will know this now.......... know it's trigger to take over and allow you deep refreshing sleep. Just as you breathe in and out.......... in and out........... night moves into day and day into night in that natural rhythm as you sleep at night and wake in the day........ as the sun rises you awake ....as the moon rises you sleep........ following the natural rhythm of sleep just as you follow the patterns of your breath.......... in and out.......... in and out........... that gentle soothing rhythm as you watch that leaf detach itself........twist and turn in the breeze, dancing in the air as it moves gently down taking you into a deep and refreshing sleep.......seeing this now.............when you go to bed at night........seeing the woodland and your journey into sleep.....a safe place...........a relaxing place.....where no-one can trouble you....expect anything of you......just allowing yourself to rest..... allowing your subconscious mind to be there....take over....giving your conscious mind time off....sleep.

Loss

Grief – The House

You are in a house of many, many rooms....I wonder what the house looks like?...Is it modern or old? How the rooms are decorated?...What room are you in now?....What colour are the walls?...What is on the floor?...Is there somewhere to sit?...So many rooms...all around you...the doors to the rooms are ajar.... the door out is always ajar...as is the door in......sometimes we stride directly out of it...sometimes we leave with hesitation.... sometimes we stumble through...sometimes we do not perhaps feel ready to leave this room as it is so comfortable...so full of delights....but the next room may be even more beautiful...even better....more exciting....more to see.....but plenty of time to see it...all in its own time....a stitch in time saves nine....allowing the time to pass.......there are people you love in this house....just in a different room...still here...still with you...just waiting in another room...waiting for you to finish what you are doing here and pass to the next room...there is no rush...they are busy enjoying the new room themselves...enjoying it....exploring it....they know you have things to do now where you are...you will not leave the jobs undone...there is time to join them in the other room...no rush...plenty of time...they are safe and secure....just enjoying new adventures in that other room....perhaps catching up with old friends and family....taking care of each other....sharing together.......you need to let them get on with what they have to do in the other room...whilst you do what you need to here.... jobs undone...unfinished here...plenty of time to join them in the next room....people who need you here and now...I wonder who is with you in this room........things to do....such a good feeling knowing they are there in the other room.....you will see them in good time...the right time.....but people here in this room need you now....need your attention now....keeping your focus on this room...the here and now....now...here....

They may have strolled out of the house into the garden for a while....the garden leads down to a beach....sloping down to the beach.......a warm day to be on the beach....the sun beating down..... ...sloughing off the overcoat...to enjoy the beach... baring the skin to the sun...warming the soul....just leaving the overcoat behind...it is not needed here in this place.....a place of relaxing...a place of resting and sleeping...that's right.....a warm...safe ....and secure place...leaving the overcoat behind... the many layers behind....not needed in this warm and comfortable place....your subconscious mind likes the stories...reads the stories and learns from the stories like a child at their parents knee... absorbing the wisdom...new learnings...new understandings....

Grief – The Barn Owl

You enter a large room with wood panelled walls..... it has a desk..... a leather desk....with a swivel chair in front of it....there are some books on one wall....there is thick carpet on the floor.... upon the desk is a blotter and an old fashioned ink pen....it is quiet and peaceful in here...then you notice something that you had missed seeing when you entered the room...a slight movement in the corner draws your attention....there is a large guilt cage over there in the corner...in the cage is an amazing barn owl...the lovely creamy feathers...the dark brown eyes...in that heart shaped face.....as you walk over to the cage...he swivels his head....looks up at you....such a beautiful and majestic bird...you sense its desire to fly....to be free from this cage....it is a beautiful cage in a lovely peaceful room...but it is in a cage nonetheless....it was born to fly...to be free to soar on the currents...the cage is on a stand...held by a hook...you wonder how heavy it is....can you lift it off.....yes.....you lift it off the hook and look around to see where you could release this caged bird....with the sad eyes...there are doors leading out onto a veranda....in the far corner of the room....you carry the bird with you...reassuring him that you are going to release him....

71

You exit the doors and find a table outside....you place the cage upon the table....open the latch, that holds the door shut and step back to the corner of the veranda...at first the great barn owl just pokes its head out of the door to the cage....swivelling right around to see where it is....then steps outside the cage....it spreads its wings wide and flaps for a moment...then up it soars into the sky...it swoops and it dives and circles around above you....it may make you think of a plane making a swooping salute....like in an old film...it is perhaps saying thank you for his freedom...then up and up he soars....getting smaller and smaller and he rides the currents of the air and seizes his freedom....

you know you have done a good thing...you imagine him flying above woodlands....soaring over fields and having wonderful adventures...from time to time you think you see him out of the corner of your eye...just a glimpse...a moment....he has come back to check you are ok....then off he goes again...following his path, his journey.

Emotional Pain – The Wound

Pain tells us that we are hurt...we can hurt in our bodies....we can hurt in our minds....our emotions...can hurt...it takes time for hurt to heal....if we have a wound....a hurt....if we have a cut... we know it will take time to heal...we do not expect it to heal overnight...we understand there is a process to healing...that healing takes time...a cut on our hand perhaps...the white blood cells rush along to help the healing....slowly new tissues begin to form .....to knit together.....and then there is new skin....it gradually....slowly....begins to heal....we do not get frustrated if we do not have a totally healed hand overnight....and we know a bigger hurt takes longer......if we broke our leg we would not expect to run the marathon the following week...even a bout of flu takes a bit of time...time to recover...we expect it...allow our bodies to heal...if we are there with a broken leg...our friends do not chide us and expect us to run....to skip and to jump....because that hurt will take time to heal...something we get to understand...

understand from quite young...we can cosset ourselves........ take care of ourselves whilst our body heals......friends signing their name on the cast....sympathy all around...such bad luck that break...so tough for you...they say....but what about that other kind of hurt...that deep and painful emotional hurt...why should that hurt be any different....why should we expect to be better overnight....the bigger the hurt....the longer it takes...no set time...but your time...the time that you need to heal...so they cannot see the hurt...but they know it is there....if they had hurt in the same way as you..... then they would know...know about the time that you need...you need to heal...be kind to yourself and accept the time...some hurts are bigger...take longer...so be patient with you...allow the healing to occur...giving your emotions the time they need...not rushing ahead too soon....just like you would allow your body to heal...postpone that marathon for a while and take care of you....whilst the bones knit together... whilst you knit together...and just like any other kind of wound... there may be scar tissue there...it is to be expected...accepted....let it be....

Other Physical issues

Immune System – The Island

See a small island....less than a mile from one side to the other....a lush island....green fields....poppies ...red...swaying....swaying in a gentle breeze.....beautiful plants around...cornflowers....the blue of the cornflowers a beautiful island...unspoiled....unspoiled by big towns...unspoiled by pollution....no pumping grey smoke....just fresh clean air....so wonderful to breathe that fresh clean air...breathing it in....that fresh clean air....no cities...just a natural island.....water all around....the island rising up out of the water....the blue....the blue of the water....rippling....rising with the current...lapping the shore......sandy beaches ....protected inlets........some mountains at one end of the island.....tall... snow-capped....tufts of heather near the base...some yellow gorse prickly....defending.....guarding one end of the island....huge rising mountains...majestic...green slopes as it rises up then that snow at the peak....there are rocks all around the shoreline of the island...protecting the sandy beaches......the rest of the shoreline ......a maze of rocks...rising up....the white spray of foam spraying up as the water swirls around the rocks...no boat can get through...nothing can get through.....through the maze of rocks....close up to the shore...no way through....no-one can board the island...except one small spot...one place through the rocks....but there is a check point there...it is well guarded....the only way in is well guarded....blocked....no unwanted visitors can get through....all the ports are closed now....safe and secure...no way in...no intruders can get through...Nothing can corrupt or poison this island...it is well protected...nothing can get through the rocks or over the sheer mountain on the seaward side....no dangerous cells....kept out....invaders repelled.....expelled..... forced back into the sea....driven off the shores of the island by the wild current...taking any invaders away....sweeping them away....all the ports are closed now....all invaders repelled.... swept away...far, far away.....you are safe....safe and secure... safe from attack....safe from invasion....all bad cells swept away... swept far out to see...the waves and current taking the invaders far away...the breeze and the current sweeping them away...all danger repelled...breathing in the pure clean air...unpolluted... undamaged...strong...seeing the beautiful secure island...all the ports are closed to invasion....dangerous cells departing, expelled out to sea...taken away by the current...swept far, far away. ....Killer K cells patrolling ....patrolling for danger.... searching out danger.....protecting.....protecting from danger.... killer cells doing their jobs...taking care of the island....seeing off danger...fighting off rogue cells...expelling them...casting them off....casting them away...sleeping soundly as you know the patrol is ongoing....all the ports are closed...immune system fighting...protecting ...expelling...flowing away far away as danger passes...the body heals and repairs...resting in the long grass....relaxing...healing...all harm expelled...fighting off all invasion....all the ports are closed...stronger and stronger... healing....healing warmth flowing through you...allowing your body to heal now...time to heal now....the island is yours now.... safely yours now...enjoying your island...going there whenever you want to.....yours to go to whenever you want to...seeing the rocks in the waters foam rising....protecting your island....your island locked up tight from invasion now as you heal.....

Vertigo/labyrinthine disturbance/balance – Aeroplane

As you continue to relax deeper now....deeper and deeper now... with each breath you take...that's right....I would like you to imagine that you are sitting in the cockpit of a small plane...... it can be any kind you want...... you may have seen what a plane cockpit looks like in a film...... or you may just imagine all the nobs and dials in front of you...... looking at the control that keeps the plane steady...... you have to align the wings of the plane with the lines to each side of the central dial....... so taking the joy stick in your hands and keeping it nice and steady.......

seeing the wings level......holding them level........ it is so wonderful to feel this sense of control........ you can shift the plane in any direction that you want.......... but the ideal for you is a straight and steady path........ keeping those wings level and gliding effortlessly forward........ safe and steady and in complete control....

You have the controls in your hands......you can feel that steadiness.... that easy gliding steadiness.....as you walk now..... no movement away from a steady gait.....an easy steady gait as you walk down the road and pass easily through the gate....feeling the level ground beneath your feet....this is not something you do not find easy now.......as you have taken control....you have the control now of your own balance.....you can walk wherever you choose now.....or run if you wish.....with that easy sense of balance.....feeling the co-ordination of your senses and your limbs.....so safe now....as you can go wherever you want with no more fears or concerns....

Because you have taken control in your subconscious mind..... your subconscious mind will now follow the commands of your conscious mind....keeping a steady straight course now......it knows what you want now and follows your commands.......as you relax into the steady rhythm of your walking, an even pace always now.....as you go wherever you want now, safe in the knowledge that you have taken control of your body now and can direct it in any way you want to...following that gentle rhythm now.....

Tinnitus – Dining out

I wonder if you have had the same experience as me when out for dinner with a friend or partner........................... you are sitting at your table and they are chatting away................you may have ordered your food.......or you may be waiting to order.........but they are chatting away........................ things perhaps you have heard before ....or they are saying things you are not much interested in ....you may look around the room............looking at the other diners............. someone at the next table says something that catches your attention............they seem really interesting..........not that you want to pry.............but you wish you could join in..........have your say...............you may disagree with their opinions........... or you may agree.................or maybe they are just telling an interesting story............................ no disrespect to the person you are with but it does sound rather interesting....................... so you tune in..................... listen in to their conversation........................... you are able to tune out from the person in front of you,....................and tune into the next table........

You can still be looking at the person you are dining with..................they think you are listening to them .... taking your focus elsewhere...........you are not listening to them..................but the person at the next table.............. you do it because you want to......want to shift your attention...................... I think we have all done this sometime..................it could be travelling on the train ....on the bus or in a café,........................... but you tune into the conversation you want to hear........................... block out all other conversations and sound...........................you know you can do this................. you have the ability to do this.....

So you can do this now........................ for yourself at will................ choose your focus, focus at will..................... take your mind where you want it to go................. take your attention where you want it to go......hear what you want to hear.........you have the choice..........you can choose your focus...............away from that hissing sound..........or that ringing sound............to something more pleasant...............a much more pleasant sound...you choose............it is up to you.........

Alternative uses for this script:

This script can be adapted to any situation where the client is being affected by noise, such as a snoring partner, or living in a noisy location.

Nausea – Body Awareness

I know you are right now focusing on your head, because the nausea is located there..... perhaps some pain too...... you are aware of the nausea locked in your head.......so you can leave it there and go elsewhere.....examine your stomach.....there is no sickness there....., just in your head..... perhaps following your attention from your stomach down your legs........there is no sickness there.............no sickness in your legs......so why linger in your head when you can go to your legs...a place where there is no sickness....or now, right down your leg.....your right leg..... into your right foot.....taking your awareness to your right foot.... or if you prefer it can be your left....left and right....right and left.....into the foot....aware of the foot and the toes there... examining each in your mind, in detail...the foot...the toes...five toes and then it is ten, all those toes, is there a sock or a shoe.... head to toe....taking yourself to the toes and letting that sickness go....you can choose to feed it....focus upon it and wallow in it, or lock it away and go somewhere else...somewhere with no discomfort...such a relief to leave the awareness of that locked up there and you go down here...drifting down to your toes...and you can do this any time you get that feeling....to avoid that feeling you do not want and focus all your energy and awareness down there...right down there.....or left down there....down in your toes....that's right....each toe in turn from the smallest one to the biggest one, on the left and on the right....choosing your focus....sending that mind to a different place.....down from the face right into the toes, via those legs left and right....

Regular Checks at the Dentist – The Experts

When you see a gymnast vault and twist and turn in spectacular way.....their skill, their training, their dedication, is there to see.....the hours they spent learning this skill, a skill they display for your entertainment...... every sportsperson learns their skill too....the footballer....the hockey player...the cricketer....they have their special sport the one at which they excel, they work hard at it..... they practice it and we see their skill......as they take control of the ball on the pitch, or perhaps hit it for a six.

I guess we all have things we are good at......things we are trained to do...a hobby...a pass time.....an experience...the writer....the artist.... the doctor....the dentist....they all have skills, skills they have honed...... some skills are there to entertain.....some skills save our lives......some rescue us from terrible pain.....then there is the fireman, the car mechanic......the nurse and the teacher...... the farmer and the fisherman, all with their part to play.

Everyone has their skill to share....something they are good at..... something they have learned and we benefit from that learning....... the hours of learning they put into that skill.......we are grateful to take our car to the garage and get it fixed.......we have to take care of ourselves to......the MOT we need sometimes at the doctor or sometimes at the dentist...... putting ourselves in their care.... they can take care of us too.......they can take away the pain..... protect us and heal us......using their skills for us, taking care of us and we can trust that skill.....learning to trust as they learned their skill...... a skill they learned to help us.......so let them practice that skill, not waiting until a disaster is there.......but getting that regular check......you do it for your car I bet.... the service, the MOT, and if the car breaks down, you call in the expert and let then practice their skill.......so seeing the dentist as that expert.......just practicing their skill, their skill to take care of you.....perhaps seeing their work in a new light......seeing what they can do for you.....maintaining and caring......having that service check.......that regular check and take care of you too.

Pacing in Life

Cultivating Patience

I wonder if you have ever heard the saying patience is a virtue, possess it if you can, seldom found in women but never in man.... not very fair I don't think.......I think women can be just as impatient as men...I guess it depends what you are doing sometimes..........I love walking out in nature........walking through the woods and sometimes I can find patience there........I wonder if you have ever seen a deer in the woods just walking quietly through the woods or perhaps leaping across a fence....... there is something very distinctive about the leap of a deer, the way they move.....so beautiful those deep brown eyes......some have that glossy chestnut coloured coat..... if you want to get near.....to get close..... they may be grazing on some grass........ you need to be patient and slow.......moving carefully and quietly...... not wanting to startle them, make them jump and then skip away........leap away before you get a chance to look at them....... to connect with them..... as they stand and nibble the grass beneath them........ it is worth it that patience you know..... you get your reward, that special moment, just for you........

Some people like fishing.....fishing with a hook and line.....they will sit for hours doing nothing at all........just watching the rod.......waiting for that twitch on the line, they do not want to miss it, that very moment........so they patiently watch and wait, wait and watch........and time passes and they get their reward..... the tug on the line the tug and the pull as they reel their fish in, patience usually gets it's reward, something worth waiting for... even if a person is slow, slow to process, not quick and alert like you.............sometimes when dealing with people you can almost see the cogs turning in their mind........ the wheels of thought turning as they decide what to do, or even do what you have asked them to do........ perhaps when it is like this, a situation like this you ....could think about a time when you were rewarded for patience...........

Hold on to that thought............perhaps teaching someone a new skill, like tennis perhaps.............when they are new to the game they will struggle to keep their eye on the ball....... hold the racket right..........be able to aim that ball to just the right place on the court......... when they get it right though.......after so much patient practice......with you watching and guiding.......all that patience, that teaching has paid off..........your patient teaching rewarded by their success........I am sure there are times you have been patient and it has paid off for you........giving people space to get it right........find their way........their words, their actions like a patient teacher......... as I am sure a teacher has been with you at times........giving you space to learn and grow......to catch up with the older ones........the ones that think they know it all although of course they never do..... know it all, they think they do but there is always a situation where we need the patience, the guiding hand.......... the moment whilst we find what we want to say or do........ enjoying slowing the pace.......I am sure you know the story of the tortoise and the hare, that old fable by Aesop........ those stories with lessons within them.........the hare ridicules that slow moving tortoise and challenges him to a race..........he is so sure of his success that he settles down for a nap and when he awakes he discovers that the tortoise has slowly and steadily made his way to the finish.......he has won, the hare was so overconfident he lost the race and sometimes, just sometimes we can learn something new........something from those around us that we feel we could teach a thing or too........ not often I grant but you never know..............so make way for the slow and wait and see if that patience gets rewarded this time..........maybe even seeing the other begin to relax....... feeling comfortable and reassured by your presence, by your wisdom, ready to learn from you..........when we are stressed the mind cannot think clearly, fight, flight or freeze........so calmly, easily, wait for the moment to pass and in time you will realise it is no longer an effort to wait and be patient it is really you, and so you can, can you not........

Pacing your life – The Race

I would like you to see yourself at the starting line for a race...... it is a long distance run....not a sprint...... along the starting line with you are various people that you love and care about....... all lined up along the starting line....joining you for the race........ I wonder how it feels...... what the weather is like...... who is there with you....... see them clearly....... hear any sounds that might be around you.......... feel the weather....... what is it like I wonder?........ imagine the feeling of the trainers on your feet........ ready to take off ....ready to run........ there is someone with a starting pistol, they will be firing it soon, yes....... off you go......... taking off on the race....... you are faster than the rest....... because you are fit........ taking off into the lead.....no injuries......at the peak of your fitness now....... in this race anyway you are up at the front......... pushing ahead...... that's right...... I wonder what the scenery is like as you pass by?.......... what can you see?....... keep on running..... how does it feel to be up there in front?......... you are pushing further ahead now...... increasing your lead, feeling the ground beneath your feet....... feeling warm now perhaps......... as you pound on........ streaking ahead of the others........feeling good at first.....being in the lead.....being first.....leaving them far behind now.........far behind you now..........you are alone at the front........ imagine and see how that feels......... right up far, far in front now.......... no one else in sight........ but I wonder how they are, those people you have left behind.......... is it still good to be at the front?....... when they are trailing........ here on your own........ without them.......... chasing ahead as they labour behind you.......I wonder if they are ok.................maybe someone may have fallen.........and you are not there to help them......... perhaps slow your pace a little............. give them a chance to catch up...............

You cannot hear anyone behind you................ no sound of plodding feet........... the ground hard now beneath your feet as you run on,...........but slower now............... slowing down now............ lonely here at the front.......... no one to share it with.......... no one to share the sights with..........no one to call an encouraging word to.................... and are they alright back there.................. slowing down now, slowing your pace down now.............. slowing it down now................. so much nicer to share the view........... perhaps even to share the victory with........... part of the team......your team......... a winning team................ hearing the feet behind you now.................... hearing them get closer now.............. calling back to hear who it is and a voice calls to you.............. good to feel them nearer now......... to know they are safe....that they are ok now..................... several feet pounding the ground now .... they begin to catch you up................ they are all there now................ the people you care for......they are around you now.......... hearing their chatter........ sometimes it has annoyed you that chatter................ but having been alone................ alone on the race............ it feels so good to hear them now.............. to know that they are there now................. running at your side.............. you can keep an eye on them.............. keep them safe........... slowing your pace now and sharing smiles with them........................ sharing the views around you with them................. slow enough to take in the view now and enjoying sharing it with them now................. not annoyed at their slowness but just relieved to be with them now................... setting your pace to their pace now................... so much better than being alone at the front with no one to share it with................feeling your muscles relax.................as you slow your pace.................. enjoying the race as you set your pace to theirs.............all the people you care for together.......... enjoying the day together.............. not needing to get there first.......... part of the team..........your team and sharing the victory with them.

Mindfulness Hypnosis

Be aware of yourself in the chair, feel it support your head now
.........feel your feet touching the floor. Take a deep breath and
exhale. Take another deep breath and exhale slowly. ....Take
another deep breath and exhale slowly again. ....

Close your eyes....I wonder if you can notice how comfortable it
feels to have your eyes closed....shutting out the light....just a
gentle glow through your eyelids perhaps.....now begin to be
aware of the sensations in your hands, are they resting on the
chair? On your legs?

Notice the sensation of touch in your fingertips,......all those tiny
nerve endings giving you, your sense of touch....... feel and think
about the feeling,........what it means to have this amazing sense
of feeling..... all the things that you can achieve because of this
sense. The sense of the support beneath you, the sensation of that
support.....maybe there is clothing touching your legs, or your
arms.....feeling all places where your body is experiencing touch.
(tie in touch with issues client is facing)

Now listen...at first focusing on any sounds outside the room....
what can you hear....focusing all your attention on sound.....the
sounds outside the room....there may be nothing....there may be
silence....or there may be a myriad of sound out there....hear
it.....but you are in here....separate from that sound....let it drift
off into the distance.....moving your focus to the sounds in the
room....can you hear any sounds within the room? Listen
carefully....focus....focus on the sound.....then moving to
yourself.....hear the sound of your in-breath....the sound it makes
as the air passes through your nose....and the sound as you
exhale....is it a little different?....the sound of the inhale.....the
sound of the exhale.....listen....listen to your body....if you go
inwards you may even hear the sound of your heart beating....that
pump, that pumps life into you....hearing the rhythm of your
body.....and beginning to reflect on all that sense brings to your

life....safety.....communication.....the joy of music.....all the wonder that sound brings into your world....our world.....*(tie in sound with issues client is facing)*

Now can you smell anything...anything at all in the space around you....we often take smell for granted.......if you really focus everywhere has a smell....good smells....bad smells...think about that sense....it can bring great pleasure....the smell of a freshly cut lawn....the smell of a flower....the smell of a perfume or aftershave you associate with someone you love....the smell of a delicious meal...it can also be a warning that something is wrong.....food going bad.....a smell of illness....focus on your sense of smell and all that it does for you each day....begin to notice when you notice smell.....*(tie in smell with issues client is facing)*

What about taste....take your focus into your sense.....if you have eaten anything recently there may be a lingering sense of taste..... or have you had a drink.....aware of your sense of taste, the saliva in your mouth....think of those pleasures those taste buds bring..... and the warnings too....take some time to value your sense of taste.....that's right.....

Now bringing your focus back to your eyes....perhaps aware again of a faint glow coming through the eyelids.....now open your eyes just for five seconds....what do you see....take it all in ....the space around you...look at the colours....look at the shapes....see how it all fits together....what a pleasure that sight can bring....more than just getting around ....your eyes closed again now....the pleasure of colour....what about a red rose....see it in your mind's eye...the wonder of it....the beauty of it....the intricacy of design...that without your sight you would not know.....(tie in sight with issues client is facing)

Thinking now about all those senses and how they enhance your life, how sometimes one will compensate for a fault in another.... all those five senses now.... ......to be valued and cherished.....not taken for granted.....

What about that sixth sense....just focus on that place between your two eyes....that place between the eyebrows....where the third eye sits....imagine...see it in your mind....aware of it.... that extra sense...give it your full attention....and listen to it.... encourage it....allow yourself to see...to know.....that deep other knowing...focus and see...and know....your instincts....*(tie in instincts with issues client is facing)*

And now it is time to relax your focus, to do nothing at all, relax now...all that work...seeing...hearing...touching...tasting..... smelling.....and knowing .....just be....just to be....be here ....now....no thinking, feeling or knowing just being...allowing yourself to be......

Relaxation

Close your eyes and clear your mind of unwanted thoughts, see in your mind's eye a picture of a woodland in summer, create the picture in your mind and step into the picture, the image, so you can see it clearly as if you are really there.

See the trees in front of you...... the brown of the bark...... the green of the leaves fluttering on the trees........ different shades of green......hear the sound of a gentle breeze ruffling through the leaves on the trees........ hear birds singing high up in the tree tops....see the branches that stretch out in a canopy above you, sway slightly with that breeze.....see the light dappling through the branches...the light shines through creating a shaft of light on the ground....are there ferns at the base of the tree?........can you see fungi there too at the base of a tree?......twigs lying on the ground.....that make that snapping sound if you walk upon them.....the earth has that damp mossy smell you associate with a woodland.....the air is warm but not too hot......see the roots of the tree.....they spread across the ground....reaching across the ground......until they go down into the soil.....all gnarled and nobly those roots......as they go deep down into the soil.... anchoring the tree....making the tree strong.....strong and deeply

rooted.....able to sway and bend with the wind and the rain.....
knowing it is held firm by its roots.....lightning and thunder may
storm around the tree....but the roots hold firm....

The tree stays safe....it keeps the birds and animals that live in the
tree safe too....can you see any birds high up in the branches.....
nesting....hiding....nurturing..... absorbing all the detail of the
woodland around you...is that a stream in the distance?.....the
sound of water...aware of all the sights....sounds....smells...even
touch sensations as you feel that warm gentle breeze brush your
skin as it sways those branches...all these sensations anchoring
you're here....here in this place....watching nature around you...
being still in the moment as you watch...hear...smell....listen...
touch...touch that gnarled bark...run your hand over the
surface....feel its rough sensations...look at all the different shades
of brown that make up that bark....there may be carvings in the
bark of the tree.....see what you see there....now imagine yourself
sitting down on the earth....with your back to the tree....look up
into the branches above you....seeing the tree from a new
perspective....a new angle....feeling the support of the trunk of the
tree at your back.....now imagine you close your eyes as you
imagine yourself under the tree....feeling the tree behind you
smelling the tree...the smell of the bark, the leaves and think
about the roots of the tree...now see yourself at one with the
tree....merging into the tree...you and the tree are at one....you
are so tall stretching up into the sky....reaching up and feeling
your roots stretching down....feeling your stretch...feeling
anchored....feeling your strength.......feeling at one with the
natural world around you....a part of it....blended into it...

Feeling that stillness at your centre...but able to sway with the
breeze...to sway with the events of your life....but safe in the
knowledge that you are strong and anchored by deep roots...roots
of family or perhaps friends....the roots that make you who you
are....rooted in nature....at one with the tree....you have become
the tree...feel yourself merge with the consciousness of the tree....
drawing on this consciousness whenever you need it....you are at
one with the earth like the tree...earthed and grounded....you

sway with the air moving effortlessly in the breeze.....alive with the fire of life....the vitality of life.....nourished by the water in the soil...the moisture in the air...nourished and fulfilled... untroubled....silent strength within.....now enjoy a few moments in the forest...using your senses...I wonder what they will tell you....what you will know now, that you did not know before?.... and now it is time to awaken and return from this journey...take a few deep breaths and slowly...very slowly become aware of your body and where you are in time and space.....open your eyes and stretch, move your fingers and toes...back in the here and now.

Pain

As pain is a perception in the mind and very much subjective, the main way to treat pain is to distract the mind from the focus on the site of the pain, any form of visualisation process will be helpful to trick the mind away from pain awareness.

Pain – Dead Sea

They say you can float in the Dead Sea......it just lifts you up and holds your body...... it just lets you float...... is it a sea or a lake?.........I think it is a lake, but they call it a sea.............lake or sea that water there allows you to float........I imagine the water to be warm........warm and soothing there......but I do not know.....I can only imagine.........that warm water, bobbing there and lying there like a bobbing cork........ feeling held and safe in that water, and the warmth soothing the back of your head........ your body so held........so supported that you can release the tension there........allow all the muscles to relax, as the water holds you and the tensions loosed.........muscles letting go......... nothing to do but allow the body to float and drift on that sea of support........ the head feeling so light.......light and at ease, with the warmth seeping in through your skin.......... your head feeling so light now.........it is the salt they say, that makes you float........ buoys you up and holds you there........salt is used for healing.........this salty lake can heal you now........saltier than any other sea.........helping you to float, to drift and to bob, and it can heal you too and that pain........just easing.........the warmth of that water, that release of tension just easing out the pain.......... can you see it go I wonder.......easing out of your head and into the water and floating away........as you lie there.......drift there.

People have been coming here for centuries to heal........for the healing powers of this water........this water that holds you and enfolds you and keeps you safe as you allow the pain to drain away........away, out into this salty water........leaving you free of tension and pain ....and just drifting, seeing yourself there, drifting........ legs out in front of you, head back in the water, but caressed by the water, soothed by the water.........the pain and discomfort soothed away..........bathing in salt water, a cure of old........to re-balance the nervous system........so you can do that now as you float in that sea........ that salty sea.......the Greeks and the Romans.......they knew a thing or two about healing.......... they understood the relaxing healing of salt sea water and you can feel it too.......washing over you........healing you, that's right......feel the tension dissolve from your neck...... your shoulders.......draining away.......the muscles in your forehead loosening up, letting go....... let the soothing water take the strain.....that pain..........drifting out and drifting away......let it go now, let it go, flowing away in the current of the water, as you allow, allow yourself to feel the support........you are supported........buoyed up by the water, so you can let it all go now.......let the pain go.......eyes closed......enjoying the gentle sway....letting the pain go.....letting that salty water....... that warm water.......heal you and you can come here when you want to......when you need this healing.........allowing your mind to take you here.

Migraine with Aura – The Warning

There is that moment..........that moment when it lets you know it is on its way........I wonder how it lets you know......... a slight flicker at the corner of your eye........a slight tremor there, just on the periphery of your vision.......a warning to you that it is on its way.........or do you get those zig zag lines shimmering there....... some people get a smell......citrus maybe, or coffee perhaps.....I wonder what lets you know it is on its way...... a glimmer.....some light, how long do you get?   a second......a minute......a few minutes even......that warning sign........like a warning bell......... those warning bells you used to get in a station, to tell you that the train was coming........ just to let you know it's on its way.......but if you get a warning........it comes for a reason.......it is giving you time......you have some time to do something about it...... to make it go away.....divert it......derail it.......stop it from landing....... send it packing......how long do you get I wonder......that moment from warning to the pain arriving....... a pain in your eye perhaps.....around your head, but you have that warning........so you can use the time......that gap in time, ...the moment you are given to stop it......sometimes just telling it will do.......have you tried that....... just telling it no......not now.......go away......I do not want this now.......I will not have that pain.......

Have you tried it I wonder.......saying no to the pain....sending it away.......or filling that moment........you could fill that moment.......however long your moment is with a thought......a calming thought......a thought that fills your attention, leaving no room..... no space for the pain to arrive in........ what will that thought be, a recollection........an image that fills your mind......a place or a person....... an experience........or a gentle sound perhaps........the crackle of a fire.....or some rustling leaves, or a sensation perhaps.....warmth.......like lying in a warm and soothing pool.......I wonder what it will be for you.......what you put in that moment to send it away.........so there is no space for the pain to fill........you have locked it out or sent it away........ either way........you are free from the pain......some people imagine those blood vessels there.......not contracting........not expanding just keeping that steady flow.......a gentle flow........ no need to speed it up, nor slow it down...... the steady beat of your heart maintaining that steady flow......but you do not have to see it........ just know it is there....... no changes occurring, just that regular flow...... so you have diverted that feeling...... that pain and the sickness, by telling it no.....you do not want it.....it can go away.........they can go away....... they will not arrive now...... you have sent them away......taken control of your body....... taken control of your mind and used that warning sign........ listened to the warning and filled that space with a different thought, or just sent it away........it is just up to you, you can do this now......try it.....fill that time.....take that warning sign and be thankful that it let you know and you can do this now.....can you not....saying no to the pain......and you can, can you not......

Phobia

General Phobia – Forgetting

We learn so much information in our lives from the minute we are born......and phobia is sometimes a learning thing......something you picked up somewhere......we usually learn these fears from a parent or........... someone around us in our childhood.....because they are there to show us the way....give us a map so to speak.....a map of the world...they give us ideas and learnings.......... or maybe for you..... it was not a person who taught you this fear.......... ...... maybe something happened and you know where it came from.......not a learning from a person but an event....an experience......will you build your response to this experience in time or cast it into the past....will you take this bad experience or throw it away........

We do a lot of learning........learning to walk...talk.....add and subtract......some learnings stay with us......and some just seem to disappear.......or perhaps it is just about forgetting....we forget many things......what you had for dinner on march the 10th three years ago.......or lunch on the 25th........the cost of a loaf of bread or a pint of milk seven years ago or maybe ten......we are quite gifted at forgetting....even at forgetting things we have worked hard to remember.......like a language at school........... those verb tables.......or logarithms and trigonometry........where did they go.......the capital of wherever..........whatever things you know you once knew but have forgotten....how about applying this learning to forget to forgetting this learning from long ago..... that fear you do not want......

We forget learnings when we do not use them ....so now is the time to stop using the learning about the fear and leave it in the past with all those other things you have learned to forget.........and if you learned this fear from a person, do you really want this modelling, this copying from the person who showed you this fear...do you want to be just like them.....or do you want to be you... free of this fear ....letting it go.....creating a new way for you to unlearn for you that fear you know you no longer want or need............however you learned it................ so from today it is gone...erased and dismissed to the very depths of your mind.....with the other learnings you have no use for..... consigned to the basement of the basement of memories that you no longer have to force yourself to remember........what a relief to let it go........

Alternative uses for this script:

This script can be adapted to deal with learned habits as well as phobias and also to target unwanted memories

Agoraphobia – The Snail

Think about a snail........a snail carries its home on its back...... ....I know you get that fact........and I wonder how that feels........ to carry your home on your back....cosy and safe..........you can stop anywhere you like .... a bit like having a camper van.......but being in it all the time....all you need around you... .....a way to be cosy and safe.......curled up in your shell........no one can get in.....just safe in your shell......wherever you roam.... that shell comes too..........so I wonder what we can do.........can we build a shell.......a shell we can bring with us.......that keeps us safe and secure.....never really out there but in here........in our own shell.......our safe shell........perhaps seeing it in your mind.......seeing your safe shell around you.........I wonder if you want to give it a colour.........that shell of yours........putting it around and you are safe and secure.......secure within your shell wherever you go........whether on the train........in the car........at the shops or in a bar..........in a restaurant or a café........a football ground or the pub........you have your shell around you........when you leave your home it comes with you....always with you and if you feel uncomfortable ....you can feel it

wrapped around you........ like being held in someone's arms....
that's right ....imagine it there around you...keeping you
safe......so you can go out now when you want to........because
you are safely within not without......safely tucked up inside that
shell......your shell......so come on out and explore......explore
from within as you go out.......one step at a time........time after
time...........time to look and to see from inside your shell.......
never out but within as you venture out......and when you venture
out.....go out there again.........it is always with you..........so
you can do it again......

Problem solving

Finding the source of a problem and fixing it – Computer Scan

As you relax deeper and deeper....I would like you to think about the fact that when you turn your computer on.....periodically it will tell you that you need to do a scan for viruses....we all know they are not biological viruses...this is computer speak for faults in the programs....things that would stop your computer running smoothly...could result in harming your computer....I am sure you have seen this at some point...it flashes onto the screen until you give it attention.... I do not know what form of protection your computer has...Norton, AVG...or some other form of protection....but if we want our computer to operate effectively we are wise to follow that instruction...if you have done it...you will be familiar with how all the document names and files whizz across the screen, so fast you can barely read them....whizzing through as it scan looks for problems....we need just the same scan from time to time....to get rid of faulty programmes....some faults could have been lurking in there for years...the problem you are having is like that warning you get on the screen that it is time to run a scan and get rid of any glitches in there...you have been alerted to the problem so time to run the scan now....your conscious mind may not be aware of the programmes and files being scanned...it is your subconscious doing the work for you... scanning through and sifting out any problems....weeding them out....getting rid of them....so that you leave here today free from that problem....your subconscious mind will have found it with the scan...we just need to let it go now...seeing the scan whirring....right through that great hard drive of your subconscious mind....letting go...rooting it out....and letting it go.....all happening beneath your conscious awareness now...and I am going to be quiet for a while to allow the process to complete.....that's right.

Chunking down problems – Crossing the Stream

Would you imagine a stream.........it can be anywhere you like......in a meadow or a wood.........a dell or near a hamlet.........so just imagine a stream........and you want to cross that stream.......now imagine you can cross that stream.......you can cross the stream because there are raised boulders across the stream making a series of steps.....steps for you to take.....steps for you to get across the stream...........there is water rushing around the edges of the boulders............. I wonder if you can see it..... I wonder if you can hear the water bubbling along.....the sparkling water racing along....you may even smell the dampness in the air as the stream rushes by....chasing along.......maybe a splash of water lands upon your skin as you stand on the bank...... as you think about crossing the stream....so what's this all about.....crossing this stream........well let's start crossing and I will tell you.....it takes a lot of concentration to step off the bank of the stream and step onto the first boulder as you find your balance there....you do not want to fall into the water.........so not thinking about anything else.....nothing else edging into your mind as you balance on the first boulder.......if you start thinking about the forth boulder you might well fall in.........you need to take it one at a time.....one step at a time.....one leap at a time.... focusing all of your attention there and you step onto the next boulder and that......that boulder takes all of your attention..... your focus.....one at a time......one boulder at a time.......you cannot look ahead or you could lose your balance and fall........ no one wants to lose their balance and fall........fall into the water......no......so keeping your attention when it is needed......... like not taking your eye off the ball......that is how it goes now.....one at a time.........so the problems you are having......not trying to tackle them all at one......not focusing on them all at once........but one at a time and giving it all of your attention......chunking it down......chunking it all down so you do not get indigestion........one bit at a time and that way you can get from one side to the other......from A to B and B to C.......do you see?.....the way you need to go........or do I need to join the dots........complete the picture......one at a time........if you tackle these problems one step at a time it will not overwhelm you...... not drown you and surround you.....taking it slow......watching your step.......mindfully watching each step you take now and your subconscious knows what to do now.....that's right.

Relationships

Releasing an old relationship – The Outfit

As you relax there...listening to my words...the sound of my voice....there was something I wanted to share with you,......I wonder if you have had this experience?....an experience that I have had before.......you walk past a shop window....there is something in there that you would love to wear....a dress...or a jacket....summer....or winter....maybe a new autumn fashion.... you really love it...you see yourself in it....imagine yourself ....imagine yourself looking wonderful in it....you may pass the shop from time to time....perhaps on the way to work.....each time you look longingly at the outfit...thinking how well it would suit you....it is expensive so you have to think about it....it hovers in your mind...how good you would look in it.....you decide you must have it.....you have just enough money....so pleased at last to be getting the outfit...you go into the shop....you decide to try it on...with certainty you pick your size from the rail...go into the changing room ....you try it on.....when you look in the mirror... it is not a bit how you saw it....the fit just is not right for you.... you cannot believe it....you were so sure that this was the one..... the one for you....but it just does not fit right....the fit is all wrong....at first you are so disappointed....you had set your heart on it...thought about it for so long...you were just so sure that this was the look for you... an assistant sees you sadly putting it back on the rail and you explain your disappointment to them... they smile and point out all the other clothes on the rail...there is so much else there....why did it have to be this particular one... but you had set your heart on it...this was the outfit for you...but after some persuasion you pick another couple of outfits from the rail...go back into the changing rooms...then try one on and look in the mirror...you look fantastic...this look is so right for you... the cut is so flattering...you feel so good as you look in the mirror...this is the one for you....you cannot understand why you had got so fixed on that other one...it was just not right for you... so you go outside and buy this new outfit...so pleased to have found the right thing for you...you just needed to open your mind to the other choices and look at all else that was there...not stay fixed on that one in the window... that one would suit someone else but was just not for you....your subconscious mind understands the stories that I tell...the meaning of my words...and can make all the changes that you need to make now...the changes to open your mind...open your mind to new possibilities...to leave the past behind...that's right....as you continue to relax.... you can now find the right person for you...the one that is a perfect fit, just right for you like a tailor made suit, they are just right for you, that's right.

Choosing your friends – Toxic Foods

There is a lot talked about today around food intolerance..... so many people become ill from eating certain foods.......there are those who cannot eat wheat and those who cannot drink milk and some people get very ill when they eat a mushroom and some people just get indigestion if they have too many onions.........we get to know our bodies and what is good for them......we find a food that makes our stomach ache........a food that gives a rash and we stop eating it...... if we know what is good for us....... we take care not to hurt our bodies when we have a choice........ when we know what is good for us........what is bad for us.....not deliberately eating the food that our body is hurt by........... but what about people........there are people that are good for us and people that are bad for us........... there are people that can be as bad for us as wheat for a celiac........people who makes us feel small.........people that make us feel angry.........people that push us into doing things that are bad for us and people who do not stretch us at all....the people who talk about us as soon as our back is turned.....the people who do not listen...or just want to claim you in a crowd....

We can take care of ourselves better if we choose who we spend time with.........who we share our thoughts with, who we give that generous gift of time to.........you have a right to choose ....a right to choose who you spend time with......avoiding toxic people as you avoid toxic foods....... you can choose it's up to you.........set up those boundaries and protect you from those people who do not listen..........those people who just want their say.......those people who take from you day after day........ time to choose and avoid that interpersonal indigestion....that's right....do it for you.....and maybe for others too...

Adoption Issues – Sycamore Seed

I wonder if you are familiar with a sycamore tree, they have these amazing seeds that look rather like a boomerang.....I wonder if you have ever seen a sycamore seed fall..........it twists and turns........spinning like a helicopter blade around and around ....until it reaches it's destination..........spinning like a top in the breeze, off it travels to start new life....... I would like you to imagine a day in the woods with sycamore trees at just the right time to release their seeds..................a plump ginger cat is stalking through the trees on his own adventure...... exploring.......... listening and looking, perhaps chasing a flicker of movement in the trees, a shimmer of movement at the edge of his vision......... so pre-occupied is he with his quest......... his chase, he does not notice the sycamore seed that is spinning down through the air towards him.........that twisting and turning..... the cat does not know that it will be contributing to the new life of a tree, changing it's whole destiny...........as that seed lands on the back of the plump cat, as the cat takes off at a bound ....it dashes through the trees.....chasing a small bird, carrying the seed with him until a low branch glances off the fur on the back of the ginger cat.............the seed is dislodged at last..............quite a way from where it's journey began and lands on the damp earth..........and slowly imperceptibly slowly that seed becomes pushed down into the ground....pushed into the soil and the rain comes down and the sun shines and all the conditions are right...........the soil is just right........so the seed grows........ shoots of life burst through the surface of the soil and then it is a small sapling and it continues to grow...........a tree it becomes a strong and healthy sycamore tree.......the product of that sycamore from far away, they are eternally connected, they share a beginning ....a belonging ....but this sycamore is in such healthy soil........it has the right amount of sunlight and nutrients up through its young and healthy roots that are pushing through the soil.......... it can take advantage of where the seed had landed, not a cramped wood jostling for space...........for healthy soil and enough sunlight, this seed landed well in just the right spot and it has deep roots now........ roots of it's own.......roots that anchor it and make it strong.......it can stand tall and strong and proud as it grows and flourishes..........part of the forest, part of the whole.......but a strong individual tree, sometimes we think they all look the same but each tree is different........ has something to offer to the forest........that great echo system of life......growth..... those trees create the oxygen we breathe......all playing their part, all from that one tiny seed spinning on the breeze and carried afar by the ginger cat.....you ended up where you needed to be to be nourished and grow...I think you know....that is something now that you can see....now you know the story of the tree....

Alternative uses for this script

New beginnings: this script can be adapted to assist someone break from the past and focus on a new beginning and on the opportunity for change, utilising the idea of themselves as a seed in new soil, with new nourishment and inputs, however, obviously any reference to the connection with the tree that released the seed should not be used in this instance, as a wholly new start needs to be emphasised.

Releasing thoughts and patterns

Mindfulness of feeling

When you get that feeling...that angry (tension/fear) feeling...I wonder where it starts.....where does it come from....bubbling up from your subconscious mind....rising to the surface...stop and notice it arrive....where do you feel it in your body....whereabouts in your body...is it in your stomach perhaps...a knotted feeling in the stomach...or like butterflies fluttering....or maybe even a sensation of.... Pain.....where do you feel it...where in your body do you feel it...a stirring feeling....joined by the thoughts...the angry thoughts....bubbling up from your subconscious mind... that reaction...the reaction to what is happening....that thought response....shooting up to the surface....like a cork bobbing up through water....breaking the surface...popping out ...that angry feeling...notice, noticing when it arrives....notice, noticing where it feels in the body.....notice if anything else comes with it...does tension come with it....does fear come with it....as you notice those feelings, notice other thoughts and sensations....is there embarrassment....did embarrassment cause the anger or anger embarrassment?...did fear cause the anger, or anger fear?....notice noticing all that you feel...freeze the moment...hold onto it...hold it still and take the time to notice it... are there other feelings?... isolation.....loss of control...

I do not know how it feels for you...only you know what is there...all the feelings that are there....not just noticing the anger...that angry feeling....but what is coming along with it... coming along for the ride....popping up to the surface...not just noticing now where that feeling starts in the body...but where does it end up?...tensing all the muscles perhaps....a bunching of the muscles perhaps....if you feel that tension bunching there.... releasing it...letting it go....how does it really feel?....what is really going on for you here?...in both your mind and your body....perhaps asking yourself why....why do you feel like this?...why?...what do you feel?....why do you feel it?....why do I have this feeling?...just pausing again for a moment...pausing to examine the feeling...the why of the feeling....i wonder if you have ever been with a child who asks why...again and again as they try to learn and understand....and every answer you give leads to another why....as they try to learn....learn from what is happening....why?...until you get to the root of it...the meaning of it...getting to the very bottom of it........when you feel the anger bubbling up...pausing...watching...watch the feeling.... pressing the pause button for a moment before you do anything ....what part of me does this anger think it is protecting?.......why did it make me feel like that?...pause a moment before ....before you react....think about the situation you are in...think about it... does it warrant this response...does it....does it really......is it a mountain...a mountain to be scaled.....or is it a molehill....just a molehill....either way...either way we can deal with it.....let us start with the molehill....just taking your foot...seeing your foot in a sturdy boot...and kicking it down...smoothing the ground.... making the ground flat...patting the earth down....so it is smooth and flat...no longer blocking your path....taking control of it..... patting the soil down...you are in control of it...of that feeling..... you know, I read about a way of preventing molehills coming back...a way to prevent the feeling coming back...it is quite simple really...you soak a rag in creosote and put it down the hole and it keeps the moles away...so they do not come back....no longer blocking your path...the path ahead of you clear now... and this particular mole will not be back to trouble you.... noticing....if you just keep noticing...

But what if it is a mountain ...a mountain in front of you..... looking at the side of the mountain, can you see any pathway....a path that others may have followed before you...you are fully equipped for the mountain anyway.....you have your ropes and crampons...picks and all the equipment you need strapped to you....so you can make your way over the mountain....scaling it...not cowering in front of it...not giving into it...but tackling it...taking it on....finding a foothold and pulling yourself up...feeling your strength as you climb up the mountain.....quite exhilarating really as you reach the top of the mountain...looking down at the valley below you...knowing you can conquer the mountain...you have all the skill and ability to conquer it....to get over the top and find your way down.....not letting the mountain block your path....not letting it beat you...knowing you can conquer it and reach the other side...leaving your pathway clear...clear of obstruction...that feeling gone away....receding...such a good feeling...such an achievement....controlling that feeling...no matter how huge it feels....taking it on....over the mountain...looking back and seeing it behind you...behind you now...conquered and overcome...overcoming that feeling...triumphant...exhilarated...and then calmer...noticing the moment it feels calmer...better...noticing the feeling has changed...the anger gone...replaced by calm...peaceful calm...notice noticing the change in the feeling.....calm now.....always noticing....the wave of emotion...surging around you...beating at the shore and then ebbing..... ebbing away...the storm has passed....and no damage is left in its wake....because you paid attention....now calm....safe...secure...holding it...holding on to the calm feeling.

Bonfire – Letting Go

As you listen to my voice...you continue to relax deeper...I would like you to imagine...see in your mind's eye that you are in a woodland....trees all around you....hear the leaves rustling above your head... look up into the canopy of trees above your head, swaying in the breeze...hear the birds singing...walking through the woods....a small stream lies ahead....see the light glinting off the surface of the stream...there is a wooden crossing over the stream....walk over to it....crossing the stream...as you reach the other side...you see that there is a large clearing up ahead of you... make for the clearing...walking into the clearing sun, brilliant above you as you step out of the trees, a huge grassy space in front of you...in the centre of which is a great stone plinth with a fire prepared within it, a huge bonfire raised up a little upon the plinth...there are steps up to it...up onto the plinth...head up there...take a look...the fire is ready to be lit...so take the matches you find on the ground, light the paper spill and light the fire....it slowly catches light...then it begins to blaze...the fire rising up in front of you...powerful... nearby on this plinth you can see someone has left sheets of paper and a pen...hear the fire crackle.... see the colours in the flames....

Now pick up the paper and write down all the things in your life that are holding you back...reasons for lack of confidence... memories you wish to shed....write it all down....take your time....there is plenty of time....I will be quiet for some moments... allow you to concentrate...write it all down....(allow about two minutes silence) that's right....when you are ready to stop writing just raise a finger on your right hand...if it is too much to do all at once...you can come back here whenever you want to....

Now picking up that paper or sheets of paper...rolling them up into a ball...scrunching them up...so satisfying...scrunching up the paper...now hurl it into the fire...watch the flames catch it... burning up the paper...freeing you from those thoughts....those feelings....those memories....such a relief....seeing the smoke rising into the air...taking it all away...you feel lighter....you feel easier...free of those thoughts and feelings...they have gone up in smoke ....disappeared....left you forever....but you can come back and release things here whenever you want to....whenever you need to....now it is time to leave this place...climbing down from the plinth....onto the grass of the clearing...head towards the sound of the stream....take that wooden bridge across the stream...back into the woodland now...hearing the sounds of the woodland now...leaving all your troubles behind you...turning your back on them....they have left you....you are peaceful and calm now...that's right.....

Mindfulness of thought

You are sitting back in an armchair in a small independent cinema..... comfy and cosy..... settling down for the big picture presentation..... relaxing down into the chair.... sinking down into the chair....here and there....sinking into the chair....what film is playing today?....I wonder what film has been playing in your head today?.....is it the I am useless story....the nobody loves me story.....let us see...the curtains covering the screen are pulling back....pulling back to reveal the screen.....what is playing?....which one is it I wonder?....are you not getting bored with this story?....the same story over and over again.....would you watch the same episode of Eastenders night after night?...settling down into your armchair to watch it yet again....or any favourite drama...is there nothing new out there?...in here....what is the theme tune to this story, some dirge like lament....so tedious this story...how about livening things up....can we change the soundtrack...put a bit of pep in it...a bit of life...in it....may be a dull story but a catchy tune might help it.....perhaps something a bit silly....something that might make you smile....

After all this story has been going round and round on that loop for so long....really time to liven it up....you are still watching the story...your story....here we go again....changing the sound track now.....I wonder what you have chosen?....what might change the feelings about this story?....I wonder how that makes you feel about the story?....your story....does it change the story at all... change the way you feel about the story....is it as clear and sharp?....I would imagine you may feel a little different about that story now....I am not asking you to get rid of the story...boring though it is...it is something you want to keep it seems...like a broken old shoe that has memories attached to it...no use at all as a shoe...but you hang on to it and that is just fine...if you want to keep that old shoe...but see it as it is...an old shoe...an old shoe for which you no longer have a use.....i am not asking you to erase the story....but just look at it in a slightly different light.....seeing it for the story that it is....just a story and not a reality.....so from the moment you wake up today....when you get those old thoughts...those old negative stories that you have carried with you ....a new soundtrack....a post script...it is up to you.....it is your story....

Regression

Regression – Flying Back to the Past

This obviously should not be used with someone with fears of planes or heights, but is good for someone practical. This will generally keep a sense of disassociation as it is a visit to the past not a becoming of the past.

I would like you to imagine that you are boarding a small light aeroplane and are going on a trip, make yourself comfortable...... the pilot is very experienced and will keep you safe..... but strap yourself in and settle down for the ride...... that's right...... relax and breathe deeply and look forward to the trip ahead of you....... see yourself gliding up..... up into the sky. .....see the blue of the sky around you and the earth below you...........

You are flying low...... beneath the clouds, so that you can see the ground clearly............... now we are heading back in time flying ....back in time to the place where you first felt this feeling........... looking out of the window look out for yourself back then.............back in time............. the very time we want to find.............. seeing the people on the ground............ seeing yourself at all ages................going back.............. that's right............ heading back in time............. seeing your past flying past you................ passing along........ gliding along........... smoothly........ floating along into the past........... when you have reached the point which we need to examine......... just raise your forefinger and the pilot will land and you can get out of the plane and visit this younger you................so that you can talk to him/her and begin to find out the source of the problem at the time it happened

That's right.......... now the pilot has your instruction, he is going to gently land the plane.............. circling around and touching down........... safely on the ground now..........now see yourself getting out of the plane and going over to this young version of you...........without disturbing yourself.......... tell me how old you are now..........

Go over to your younger self, tell them that everything is going to turn out alright......... they are at the beginning of the story and it gets better...........offer love and support......... be their friend................(Give them time to do this reassuring them as they do) That's right

If someone else has hurt you at this time, find them.............they will be there and tell them how they have hurt you.......... if someone has let you down........ tell them........... take this opportunity to have your say, in a way you were unable to do back then. You have a voice now......a chance to say what you need........take this time now....................time to have your say.........(Give them time to do this reassuring them, as they do what they need to do) That's right.

Now let go of the associations of pain and hurt with this time................ leaving it in the past where it now belongs. ... That's right.................the emotional response that you had to this situation, is no longer there, as you have said all you needed to say to the people around you at that time and given care and support to your younger self. ....Now return to the plane and get comfortable again for the ride home...........heading back to the here and now, so see yourself safely landing on the runway, a job well done.......... feeling so good to be going back home, heading back home........... back to where you belong. Flying along.........seeing yourself returning to the present, returning to the now........... your life now.......... safe and secure.......... feeling aware that you have laid some problems from the past to rest at last, having visited your past.......... given yourself the comfort you need and back now...... landing in the present, landing safely.......... stepping out of the plane....... seeing yourself greeted by someone now, who loves you, greeting you back........... welcoming you home. That's right......... safely home...(go to trance termination reinforcing the change that has been achieved)

If the client has multiple issues then you may visit various times using the same format.

Regression – Autobiography

This script encourages a complete regression, so be certain that your client is ready for this experience, it is designed to induce an abreaction.

I would like you to imagine you are in a beautiful old house......... a house with many rooms...... find your way to the library in this old house........... there is a fire crackling in the grate..........hear that comforting sound......... feel the warmth of the fire.... so relaxing........... there is thick carpet upon the floor........... so soft........... a comfortable armchair in front of the fire........... sitting back in the armchair.......... relaxing............. now see on the surface of the table by the chair......... a copy of a book....... it has your name on it..... it is your autobiography.......... it is the story of your life so far..

Pick the book up and start flicking through the pages............ look at the titles of the chapters and go back to the point where you first had this feeling........... the feeling you are here to look at,.............start reading the story, see the images of the story of your life at that time become clear and sharp in your mind, back to you at that time now.......... see what you are seeing clearly and then step into the picture. ....go right back to that time, stepping into the story and look around you, be inside the memory.......... looking out at the world, as you once did......... I wonder what you are wearing......... what kind of shoes you have on your feet........ how strange it feels at first to be small again.

Back to your childhood, seeing the world around you and using all your senses to anchor you there......... but you are quite safe, because you can leave whenever you want to........ that's right, this is just a visit......... but feeling what it is like again......... hearing what you are hearing and seeing what you are seeing........... as if you are really there, inside the memory........ reliving that time....... but safe because I am with you........ I will not leave you........ I am with you all the time.........just think and feel as you did then........ you can say it out loud if you want to.......... without disturbing yourself.......... let any feeling you have come out once and for all...............release all that emotion......... it is safe to do so now, as it was not safe to do so then.........for you...........I am here with you now, you are not alone.

You are safe and protected. ......you do not have to keep those feelings in anymore..... feeling the relief, of letting those feelings you have kept inside for so long......... letting them out so that they cannot affect you any more........ free from those painful thoughts and feelings, as you finally release them once and for all......... that's right............If there is anyone in the story you want to talk to and tell them how you feel, tell them now........ as you were unable to do so back then.......... tell them how it has felt........ if they hurt you, or let you down, this is them then not now............it was them then, that hurt you or let you down, so talk to them at the right time and let it all out. ....That's right.........you are safe now. ....safe and secure, free, free from all that trapped emotion........ you have said how you felt...........you have told them all......... you are free now..........

You have released all that emotion and pain.......... you have had your say and you are now free of the past and its effect on you........ and now it is time to return, returning back, moving back through the pages......... feeling the pages turn in your hands now, leaving that memory behind now, it dims into the past as you have left the impact of that experience behind you,.......... back to the current day, as you turn through to the beginning of the book..........to the moment now.......... holding the book in your hands......... in that room and now ....(Now visualise a safe place with them perhaps something that you have agreed in advance)

Regression – The Tardis

I wonder if you watched Dr Who as a child? .....Or you may watch it now...it has changed a lot since those early days....with daleks that looked like they were made on Blue Peter....not the high tech special effects of today......I wonder who was your favourite Dr Who? John Pertwee...Tom Baker ...Peter Davison.... all so different....but all are THE DOCTOR.....what I loved most was the Tardis...that amazing old Police Telephone Box....so old fashioned....so distinctive....that noise it used to make to let you know it was about to transport in time.....i can still hear it now.....I wonder if you can..........that Tardis made me think of old fashioned films...back in the past.....but when you stepped inside...so much space....a wonderful concept...a wonderful imagining....I so wanted a trip in the Tardis....a way to go back and forward in time....if you could go back in time...visit something back in time....somewhere that you want to feel different about...change the way it feels....I wonder how old you would be if you went back...when and where you would like to visit....let us imagine that Tardis is in front of us....that sign saying police over the top...no-one is around so you can step inside...how does it look inside? ...big I guess....stretching out... so much space...did you know that the word Tardis is in the dictionary now, to mean deceptively large?....well you are in that deceptively large space...look at the controls....they say the Tardis is sentient...it knows and thinks things...I think it knows where to take you...no need to do anything...just take a seat and enjoy the ride...is it making that sound? That familiar sound...we are on our way....back to that time where you first had that feeling you want to release...change...see in a different light...a softer light....a comfortable light.....are you there yet?....raise a finger to let me know when you have reached your destination...that's right....safely landed now...

So time to step outside....step into the memory...you are just visiting...you can jump into the Tardis whenever you want to and it will take you home...you are secure here...the Tardis will take care of you...whisk you home when you want to...just visiting now...go over to your younger self....let them know how it feels to visit...let them know, that this time will pass for them...become a distant memory...a memory that you can now see in a new light....you can suggest what they might want to do...what will make them feel better...give them love and support...be the friend they needed back then...someone to talk it over with...let them know this time will pass and they will be free....as you are free now...free of the bad feeling associated with this time...because you can see things differently now...if there is anyone around you would like to tell how it felt back then...a parent...a friend...a family member...seek them out...say the things you were unable to say then...let them know what it felt like for you...have our say...if there is no-one you need to talk to, just give support to the younger you...be their best friend...let them know some good bits lie ahead...when you are ready to leave this place let me know by raising your finger...that's right...ready to go now... say your goodbyes and let the younger you know you can come back if you are needed at any time...step back into the Tardis and it knows when you are ready to go....that noise starts again...on your way to another time...are you ready to come back to now...as you raise a finger...if you want to we can stop off on the way....you may want to visit a good time...shall we do that...raise your finger once if you would like to visit a time, when you felt really good (hopefully the client will concur, just bring them back to now if not)....

The Tardis knows where to take you...stopping now and getting out...seeing the fun and pleasure you had at this time...you may even want to smile...go up to the people around you, tell them how good this time was...how much you appreciate it...how much you appreciate them....enjoy those good feelings and amplify them...bring those good feelings back with you in the Tardis...I am going to be quiet for a moment to allow you to really enjoy this experience...(allow about two minutes silence)

now it is time to return to the Tardis...hop in and settle down...
time to return back to the present...bringing with you the present
of new feelings about the past...good feelings resolving bad
feelings...good times helping the bad times...having had your
say...and given your younger self, the support they had craved...
travelling back now....and when you feel the Tardis has touched
down in the now....raise your finger...that's right...soon it is time
to awaken...and return from your journey.

Sexual Matters

Erectile Disfunction – Back Seat Driver

I wonder if you have had the experience of driving your car.........
there is someone sitting there beside you in the passenger
seat.......... or in the back behind you and they keep telling you
what to do.......... they tell you the best way to go.............or let
you know there is a red light up ahead.....like you hadn't seen it
already........ have you seen the lorry turning?..........the cyclist
up ahead?......... I know a better route.......... if only you turned
left instead of right.......... I would have got into the left hand lane
if I were you.......on and on it goes........they always know best
whatever you do.......does this sound familiar I wonder.....or
have you been in a car when another has suffered.....suffered the
back seat driver..........I call it the back seat driver syndrome you
know........no matter how hard you try they distract you and
perhaps..........just perhaps make the journey a less safe one
because they do not let you get on with the job.......... always
distracting you with inane observations........ or things you
already know.........now why I am reminding you of this you
wonder?.......now I often blame the subconscious mind for some
of its entrenched patterns....it's learned behaviours........ but in
some situations it does know best..........and the conscious mind
can be just like that back seat driver.......nagging you with
distractions..........raising fears where there aren't any and taking
you away from the job in hand.........muddying the waters.........
leading you down blind alleys......... so the purpose of this story
is just to remind you that sometimes your subconscious does
know just what to do.......... it is time to turn down the chatter of
the conscious mind.............let your subconscious get on with the
job....go *to direct problem*

Alternative uses for this script:

This script can be adapted to any situation where over-thinking will effect the outcome, such as playing an instrument or indeed driving, allowing the subconscious mind to get on with the job at hand whatever that job might be.

Fertility – Nature Doing its Job

Nature is an amazing thing..........i have been reading a book about trees......about how the forest seeds its new trees............ when the soil is ready........it has the perfect balance of nutrients and water..........it is well aerated and there is shade from a nearby tree so the soil does not dry out but there is enough sunlight so that when the tree grows it can take nourishment through its leaves................the temperature is just right.......... so now the soil waits for the seed.........a passing bird lands at just the right spot......helping the forest....... the seed falls onto the ground................just right there under the shade of the tree..........but with enough sunlight to enable the tree to nourish itself .... not enough sunlight............. to dry out the soil............. in that rich and healthy soil.......... it works its way own into the earth from the surface............ slowly........making its place there in the earth..........drawing the nutrients in.......... it rains.....the rain soaking into the ground.........reaching the seed nestling there...........it is safe and secure......it is in just the right place..........the seed can begin to grow............

your body knows how to ready itself for the new life to grow........ it understands the meanings of my words and the stories that I tell.........nature knows what to do.......you can trust it.........it brings us the abundance of trees and flowers........and created a delicately balanced eco system with butterflies and bees............ everything having a role........a purpose.........the whole of nature is gearing around procreation...........keeping every species going........so nature is on your side.............you are ready........ your body is healthy........nourished and prepared.....when the seed arrives..........you will nurture it............ready now for the new life to arrive.......to settle.......to lodge to grow welcoming the life within......the new life within.......just as that rich brown soil welcomes the seed......you see nature knows what to do........ it will help you........create new life within you.........you have chosen this path........prepared the way....it is welcome.....this new life.......like a bird preparing a nest for the new arrivals...... you have done what you need to do......looking after you.......the loving preparations you have made.....

the plans you have drawn up........leading you towards your goal....new life......new beginnings....stirring within you.......i wonder if you will feel that instant...that very moment as the fertilisation happens......that spark of life....that magical moment.......as the new life begins inside you.....that creation...... new beginning.........welcoming.......treasuring......... nurturing..........you know what to do now......you have always known what to do.....all I am doing is reminding you.....and perhaps now you could take a moment or two to imagine having your first baby scan.....seeing the reality within you.......knowing the baby is there and you are taking care......the months pass....... it is nearly time.......you have everything ready......and before you know it they are there in your arms......new life.....new beginnings.........your conscious mind has made this decision to create new life......your subconscious understands this too now.......is working with you to ensure........ensure the conditions are just right......ready........the nest prepared........ your body healthy......fit and nourished.....allowing the baby to grow and develop within you ....so there is no need to worry or stress as all is prepared.......you can rest and relax and allow nature to take its course.......

Stutter

Stutter – The River

As you relax deeper and deeper..... become aware of a flowing river..... flowing smoothly......see the river in your mind.....no obstructions..... no boulders in the way..... the gentle flow of the river..... taking you with it....the sun glinting off the surface of the water..... hear the water flowing....flowing along on the river..... so relaxing.......going with the flow.... becoming part of the flow....drifting....flowing easily now....words flowing easily now.....no obstructions......flowing as your conscious and subconscious mind work together now....a clear focus....like crystal clear water...seeing what you want to say...holding it and releasing... releasing the words....in complete control.....crystal clear....like driving your car...cruising along the motorway... cruise control set...nothing to do but relax and enjoy the ride.... an empty open road ahead of you....

You do not have to think about it...no need to think about it...the words come easily.....forgetting to remember that it was ever difficult....putting all thoughts of past talking behind you....you open a new chapter now...a new chapter in your life now....where you look forward to talking...feeling the joy of talking...sharing your thoughts and they flow out easily as that stream gently flows....so comfortable now....that's right...

Stutter – The Talking Stick

Long ago at gatherings of groups of people and in some traditional cultures today.... when someone wants to speak they are given the talking stick...the stick gives them permission to speak....it gives them confidence to speak...it gives fluidity of speech....you can take hold of the talking stick when you want to speak...imagine gripping it in your hands...imbued with all that tradition and magic of the past...holding the stick in your hands you have all the power...the ability...the confidence...to speak freely...allow yourself to take hold of the talking stick....hold the power and speak....

People pay attention to your words ....give you their time to listen....take the control into your hands now....take the talking stick and speak your truth....you will be heard...you have permission to speak....this is your time...take it...seize it.....speak it out loud.....you are free to speak...the freedom of speech is yours....seeing it in your mind that stick....holding onto it and you will speak freely and easily.

Poems to Use in Therapy

Poetry is a rich source of metaphors, we can read a poem to a client and then take the metaphor within the poem and develop it to deliver the message we want the client to hear. We even find metaphors within Literature becoming common references, such as Shakespeare's "green eyed monster" to describe jealousy.

One of my favourite poems to help with depression is "Not Waving but Drowning" by Stevie Smith, this short poem can give the client a sense of being understood, that someone really appreciates how it feels to cry for help and feel that no one is listening. The poem utilises the common idea of being "out on one's depth" this useful and universal metaphor within the poem can be developed by the therapist to deliver the message that you are going to help them to swim, or you are throwing them a lifebelt, rescue is at hand.

W H Auden's Funeral Blues depicts the absolute nature of loss, the totality of the emotional wipe out is referenced by the comparison of the deceased loved one with the four points of the compass, leaving nothing behind due to the loss. The utter despair is enhanced by the use of devices like alliteration, personification, metaphor and heroic rhyming couplets. The grieving listener's mind cries out, "yes" that is just how it feels, someone understands, someone, somewhere understands my pain. We can then carefully and gently lead them out of the dark having made that connection, not in a patronising way but a way that is delivered right to their core, we can ask them, "when will they notice that first star blinking back to life again?" Thus using the metaphor created in the poem to shut off the stars and developing it to create therapeutic benefit and also implanting the trigger that when they see the stars at night, it will begin to re-engage them with the world.

We can use humour within poems to help someone to reflect on a behaviour, using the humour to bypass resistance. An example of this could be Phyllis McGuinley's poem "Reflections at dawn", in this poem McGuinley uses some wonderful metaphors to describe her need to keep talking in social situations, whether it is appropriate or not she has to talk. The most eloquent of these metaphors is comparing the conversation topic to a horse galloping by, which she has to grab hold of and essentially mount the horse and run with it, this also utilises the old concept of our mouth running away with itself. This vivid imagery combined with a universal metaphor reaches into the client's subconscious, it is light-hearted and gentle but probes the question as to why the person needs to talk and cannot sit comfortably within themselves, leading ultimately to an increase of self awareness and self worth.

Below is a list of poems that can be a rich source of metaphors to be developed for your clients, a starting point to explore this rich seam of therapeutic metaphor:

Depression

Ode to Melancholy – John Keats

Not Waving but Drowning – Stevie Smith

The Journey – Mary Oliver

Wild Geese – Mary Oliver

There is a Pain so Utter – Emily Dickinson

Weather the Storm – Adyan Rotica

Pain – James Grengs

The Pain – Rhiannonm Franklin

Hope is a Thing with Feathers – Emily Dickinson

Grief

Remember – Christina Rossetti

Funeral Blues – W H Auden

Grief – J Sheba Ananhandi

But you Didn't – Merrill Glass

A Life – Sylvia Plath

The Division of Parts – Anne Sexton

Echo – Christina Rossetti

Do not Stand at my Grave and Weep – Mary Elizabeth Fry

Family

At Peckham Rye – Clare Pollard

I Do, I Will, I Have – Ogden Nash

Fifteen, Maybe 16 Things to Worry About – Judith Viorst

On the Pulse of Morning – Maya Angelou

I Remember, I Remember – Philip Larkin

Digging – Seamus Heaney

Mother to Son – Langston Hughes

A Father to his Son – Carl Sandburg

Anxiety

6am Thoughts – Dick Davis

Panic Attack – Jamie M Picket

Fear – Raymond Carver

When Strangers Dictate your calm – Naomi Hon